D0580190

RECRUITING:

HELP AND HOPE FOR FINDING

VOLUNTEERS

WRITTEN BY ELLEN E. LARSON
ILLUSTRATED AND DESIGNED BY SANDY WIMMER

STANDARD
PUBLISHING
Cincinnati, Ohio

BETHEL SEMINARY WEST
LIBRARY
6116 Arosa Street
San Diego, CA 92115-3902

Unless otherwise indicated, all Scripture is taken from the HOLY BIBLE: NEW INTERNATIONAL VERSION®. Copyright © 1973, 1978, 1984 by International Bible Society. Used by permission of Zondervan Publishing House. All rights reserved.

The "NIV" and "New International Version" trademarks are registered in the United States Patent and Trademark Office by International Bible Society. Use of either trademark requires the permission of International Bible Society.

Edited by Karen Brewer

The Standard Publishing Company, Cincinnati, Ohio
A division of Standex International Corporation
© 1994 by Ellen E. Larson
All rights reserved
Printed in the United States of America

01 00 99 98 97 96 95 94   5 4 3 2 1

Library of Congress Cataloging-in-Publication Data

Larson, Ellen E.
    Recruiting : help and hope for finding volunteers / Ellen E.
Larson.
        p.   cm.
    ISBN 0-7847-0232-2 :
    1. Christian education--Teacher recruitment. 2. Lay ministry.
I. Title.
BV1530.L37   1994
268' .3--dc20   94-11015
                                                                  CIP

Contents

Section 1
You, the Recruiter

Have you been asked to find new teachers and assistants for the Christian Education Department of your church? Did you say:

"I'd be happy to help, but I'll need some guidance. Do you know about some resources to help me get started? What do I do first? How do I know who to talk to?"

Then this is the book you are looking for!

Section 1 describes the ministry of recruiting and explains the first steps for a new recruiter. Here are the biblical priorities and guidelines for contacting potential teachers.

You, as the recruiter, are a part of God's plan to use His people to do the work of the ministry. Be blessed as you serve God and His church!

THE BIBLE AND RECRUITING

"I'm excited about my new responsibilities as a recruiter. But will I have to talk people into doing something, some kind of ministry? I don't think it's my place to convince someone how to serve God. Aren't people supposed to offer willing service to the Lord and His work?"

You have accepted the challenge of recruiting new teachers and workers for your church's education department. But isn't this a personal decision between the individual and God? Is there a place for recruiting?

What does the Bible say?

Matthew provides guidance to us as recruiters. We *are* called to be a part of God's plan of recruiting, and, in addition, Jesus shows us the proper attitude.

Jesus went through all the towns and villages, teaching in their synagogues, preaching the good news of the kingdom and healing every disease and sickness. When he saw the crowds, he had compassion on them, because they were harassed and helpless, like sheep without a shepherd. Then he said to his disciples, "The harvest is plentiful but the workers are few. Ask the Lord of the harvest, therefore, to send out workers into his harvest field" (Matthew 9:35-38).

Recruit for the Right Reasons

Jesus had compassion on the crowds, "because they were harassed and helpless, like sheep without a shepherd."

When your second grade children need a new teacher, do you find just anyone who is willing to be with the kids, or do you prayerfully search for the individual who is concerned about the spiritual development of seven-year-olds?

Are you recruiting a new teacher for the teenagers because there is no one to work with them, or because the teenagers must be taught about how God feels about them?

Do you consciously concern yourself with the helplessness of each individual if he or she does not have someone to teach them? Having compassion, sharing in Jesus' attitude toward those who need a teacher, changes the task from basic recruiting to sharing in God's desire to save the lost.

See Recruiting as Continuous

"The harvest is plentiful but the workers are few."

There always will be a need for more people to minister God's love. Considering the hurts and concerns of those around us, the harvest is more plentiful than ever, and the workers are still few.

Since most teachers and assistants are giving extra time—what's left after work and home responsibilities—they are often limited. There will always be a turnover in the teaching staff. Recruiting is not just a temporary task, accomplished once, and then completed. Accept the fact that you must make recruiting a top and continuous priority. This always should be an ongoing part of the ministry leadership in your church. Although the workers are few, Jesus told us what we are to do about that.

Pray

"Ask the Lord . . . to send out workers."

As recruiters, our specific God-given responsibility is to pray. Before God sends out teachers for those who need them, we are called to prayer. This prayer makes the difference. God calls and gives the abilities for the ministry needs in your church, but He asks you to do the praying.

As you recognize the importance of this part of the recruiting process, look for ways to have others join you in prayer. Here are a few suggestions:

Prayer Committee: Establish a prayer group that is formed specifically to pray for new leaders. This group should meet regularly, not just once a year or when new teachers are needed. God is always calling workers, and we need always to be praying.

Prayer Postcards: Periodically mail postcards or letters to the congregation asking for prayer for new leaders and teachers.

Know That God Does the Calling

Prayer Partners: Organize the parents of children's and teen's classes to pray for the current and potential teachers of their children.

Share Answers: Share the answers to these prayers publicly. We are all encouraged to continue to pray as we see God at work in His church.

"Ask the Lord of the harvest, therefore, to send out workers into his harvest field."

God calls people to teach and serve others in His church (see 1 Corinthians 12 and Ephesians 4:11-13). Rely on the truth that God loves His people and is even more concerned about who is ministering to them than you are.

The Bible frequently speaks about our responsibility to teach others through our love and service. God calls each of us to be ministers for Him. Our task as recruiters must be to pray with Jesus' compassion. As we are consistently faithful in our responsibility, God will send the workers.

DEFINE RECRUITING

What do you know about the words "recruiting" and "recruiter"? Check the statements with the best description.

I think *recruiting* is:
1.__ convincing someone to do something he or she would rather not do.
2.__ always a problem. There aren't enough leaders to go around.
3.__ embarrassing. No one responds to appeals for leaders.
4.__ an opportunity to help fill one's God-given need to serve.

A *recruiter* should:
5.__ pray frequently for specific guidance.
6.__ look over the congregation to see who isn't currently involved.
7.__ complain a lot about the lack of volunteers.
8.__ focus on the fact that this is God's church.

Did you check 1, 2, 3, or 7? If so, we need to talk. You are going to need extra help!

Number 6? At least this is a beginning.

Numbers 4, 5, or 8? Look forward to some effective recruiting!

The dictionary describes a recruiter as one assigned "to increase or maintain the number of [persons to complete the task] . . . or to secure the services of [those persons]."

Being a recruiter in a church can be a demanding challenge. You will be asking people to do something they may not be trained for, to give of their extra time, and to give without monetary or immediate reward.

As a recruiter, you will:

- be a public relations person for the ministry of teaching God's Word.
- share excitement about Christ and talk about the opportunity to educate the believers and win the unsaved.
- let people know that ministering as a teacher is an effective, life-changing opportunity.

Read 1 Corinthians 12:12-27. You are working in God's church and He expects everyone to have a part in it. In fact, He has given each of us the ability to make a significant contribution to His body. This means that God has provided the teachers for the people within your church. Your role as a recruiter becomes that of an encourager. Find beginners who haven't used their gifts, become a talent scout and a placement service. As you consider how to help each person move into active service, remember that God does the calling and the gifting.

The apostle Paul gives us recruiters a word of encouragement. We are also a part of God's plan, one of those He has called to be a part of His church: "The one who calls you is faithful and He will do it" (1 Thessalonians 5:24).

Consistent prayer is the first and most significant step in your recruiting efforts. God is very interested in those who will be teaching His learners, so talk to Him about this, first and often. This is the method God has chosen for our communication with Him, and it is essential to us as His followers. Prayer fits in with your recruiting ministry in several ways.

Many of us find that recruiting is more challenging than we originally perceived. It should be easy to ask people to donate time to God's work. However, as the challenge becomes greater and there is little response, it is very easy for us to be discouraged.

Ask God to help you remember that calling people into ministry is His responsibility. Although we need to approach people to present opportunities for ministry within the church, Matthew reminds us that our true responsibility is to pray (Matthew 9:37, 38).

Daily prayer brings us into a relationship with God that focuses on who God is and what He is doing, rather than depending on our own wisdom and ideas. As we continue in prayer, the Holy Spirit fills us with God's love for the church and a sensitivity for His direction.

> And God placed all things under his [Christ's] feet and appointed him to be head over everything for the church, which is his body, the fullness of him who fills everything in every way (Ephesians 1:22, 23).

We each are a part of God's church and need to look continually to him for guidance. Pray that you will have God's heart, and the fruit of His Spirit will be shared with those you are recruiting.

PLACE PRAYER AS THE TOP PRIORITY

Pray to Be Able to Return the Responsibility to God

Pray to Know God's Vision and Will

Pray to Be Directed to Those God Is Calling

Ask God to lead you to the persons He is speaking to about becoming involved in the educational ministry of the church. Obviously, a natural leader and/or a professionally trained teacher would be an asset in any classroom. However, when God is calling someone with less obvious skills, we often overlook him or her.

Most of us can remember our first opportunity for leadership. Probably someone who was led by God saw beyond our obvious capabilities. Pray that God will use you in the same way in another's life. Ask for specific guidance to be led to the one in whom only God sees the potential. Guard against being blinded by human limitations. Only through prayer is it possible to accept God's desire to use someone who does not yet exhibit all the necessary qualifications. Opportunities may be lost if we do not ask for the Holy Spirit's leading. "It was he [God] who gave some to be . . . pastors and teachers" (Ephesians 4:11).

Pray for Excitement to Share With Others

It is thrilling to be a part of the work of the almighty God. It is an honor to talk to Him and to contribute to the fulfillment of His plan on earth. Sometimes, as we experience difficulty recruiting teachers, it is hard to be excited about the work of the ministry.

Ask God to give you His excitement, even if your recruiting is not going well. Your joy comes from Jesus Christ and the salvation He offers, not from anything within ourselves. This source of joy never changes.

As recruiters we need the Holy Spirit's excitement to share. Few are willing to become involved with a discouraged, unhappy group of teachers. Pray for Romans 15:13 to be true for you: "May the God of hope fill you with all joy and peace as you trust in him, so that you may overflow with hope by the power of the Holy Spirit."

As you accept the challenging responsibility of recruiting new teachers and assistants for the Sunday school, make 1 Thessalonians 5:17 your recruiter's motto: "Pray continually." As this becomes our priority, God will do His work of providing the teachers for His church.

APPLY THE GOLDEN RULE

Do you remember when you were the one being recruited, wondering where and if you fit into the ministries of the church? Did you know then what opportunities you had and what they involved? Even if you were never one of the recruited, the Golden Rule can affect the way you locate new teachers and assistants.

The Golden Rule is used in many contexts, not just in the church. Taken from Christ's teaching in the Sermon on the Mount, this popular adage helps us relate to others by considering our own needs and interests.

"Do to others as you would have them do unto you" (Matthew 7:12 and Luke 6:31) is the common way of expressing this valuable advice. When put into practice this rule for living improves all situations, including recruiting.

Imagine yourself as the one not yet involved in any area of ministry in your church. How would you best like to be approached and challenged to minister? Imagine the interests, fears, concerns, and attitudes you would have. What recruiting methods would bother you or discourage you from volunteering your time and abilities? Your answers to these questions may show you how to develop more effective ways of recruiting people into Christian education ministry.

Carefully consider how you would respond to the following:

"If I were being recruited, I would respond *favorably* when . . . ."
"If I were being recruited, I would like to *know* . . . ."
"If I were being recruited, I would be *frustrated* by . . . ."

Although every congregation includes different personalities, as individuals we have more similarities than differences. The Golden Rule suggests that what is important to you is also important to others. How you would ideally like to be recruited should show you how to establish recruiting relationships. Create your own list of ideal methods, and then put them into practice. Here are some possible responses to help you get started.

If I were being recruited:
1. I would want to know as much as possible before I made a commitment.
2. I would want someone to ask me if I have considered teaching to be a possible ministry for me. Sometimes others can spot abilities in a person that he or she isn't even aware of. If someone took time to help me explore the possibilities, I might discover an area of ministry I hadn't thought about.
3. I would want to be able to ask questions without being pressured to become involved.
4. I'd like an easy way to tell about my previous experience. I'm more comfortable filling out a form or writing a note to indicate my teaching interest and successes.
5. I need to know there is respect for the other commitments in my life, especially if I don't have much time to give.
6. I have difficulty talking to someone I don't know.
7. I would need someone to help me with training before I start.

Use some of these suggestions to develop a list that suits your situation. As you decide how you would like to be recruited, you can devise a workable plan.

Periodically go back to the Golden Rule and apply it again to your recruiting approach. Sometimes our methods are influenced by our needs. However, we are doing God's work. We cannot lower our standards, even when the need is the greatest. God has provided guidelines for us, and we must follow them carefully. We must use the Golden Rule, "for this sums up the Law and the Prophets" (Matthew 7:12).

Recruit as you would like to be recruited.

KNOW WHOM TO RECRUIT— IS WILLINGNESS ENOUGH?

What kind of person do you look for when you start recruiting new teachers for your Sunday school? Is a willing adult all you need, or are you looking for other qualities? How do you maintain a standard for teachers?

These questions are all a part of recruiting, and they need to be considered as you ask new people to be teachers. As the administrator of your church's education department, you have a significant responsibility. When you recruit someone to be a teacher you are appointing that person to a place of influence. The Bible reminds us that God holds teachers accountable: "Not many of you should presume to be teachers, my brothers, because you know that we who teach will be judged more strictly" (James 3:1).

Prayerfully consider the basic standards before you begin looking for more teachers. Even with room for individual Christian growth, some requirements need to be met before a person is qualified to teach others. Write down commitments that apply to your group. See "Standards for Staff" on page 12 to help you develop a list of standards. Share this list with those interested in becoming teachers.

Spiritual Commitment and Attitude

Anyone who wishes to become a teacher or leader must have made a commitment to Jesus Christ as Lord of his or her life. The goal of Christian education is to teach and encourage others to grow in their relationship with Christ. Leaders must be firmly committed to Christ before leading others. This commitment should include weekly church attendance.

Occasionally someone who is not a Christian may want to become a part of the teaching team. This usually happens when a child comes to Sunday school regularly with a friend, and the parents offer to help out. Their offer provides an opportunity to explain the criteria for teachers and present the gospel to them. Welcome them into the classroom to assist if it seems appropriate, but don't let your need for teachers lower the standard for a committed Christian to be the lead teacher.

As the recruiter, you also need to discuss with each potential teacher his or her attitudes about private devotional time, and an ongoing spiritual relationship with Christ.

Being a student of God's Word and growing in relationship with Christ and each other are minimum requisites for all teachers, not just new ones. Teachers teach with their lives as well as their words and are models to their students, whether they know it or not. As representatives of Christ, we must have high personal standards.

A good starting point for discussion is to ask, "How did you become a Christian?" or "Tell me how you first heard about God and His love for you?" Then ask, "Where do you feel you are now in your walk with God." Listening to a person express his or her spiritual journey helps you know how it will be expressed in the classroom.

Teachable

A potential teacher must also be a student, open to being taught, and willing to be a part of a team. Of course, the church is responsible for

STANDARDS FOR STAFF

"I, _____, have committed my teaching to Jesus Christ. I recognize the responsibility I have undertaken in this position of influence. I commit myself to being faithful in this ministry as unto the Lord."

1. Weekly:

I will attend at least one adult worship service each week.

2. Daily:

I will maintain personal devotional time and become as involved as possible in the personal lives of my students. I will pray regularly for each student and his or her family, and make contact as soon as possible with any who are not present in class. I will keep personal record sheets up-to-date.

3. Each Class Session:

I will attend the prayer fellowship for all teachers, held in Room 10 of Tower Circle 9:00-9:15 a.m. Sunday. I will be in my classroom at least fifteen minutes before starting time. I will use this preclass time for individual Bible learning activities and to minister to students personally.

4. Monthly:

I will attend at least 10 out of 12 Christian education staff fellowships this year. Meetings are held the second Tuesday of each month, 7:00-9:00 p.m., and are very important for inspiration and instruction, as well as planning for the coming month's lessons.

5. As needed:

I will contact my department superintendent as soon as possible when I know I will be absent to allow time to arrange for a substitute.

6.

I commit myself to be faithful to this ministry for a minimum of one year (September through August).

Signed _____

Date _____

providing training. A recruit doesn't need to possess all the teaching skills before beginning, but he or she must evidence a desire to be trained and grow in proficiency as a teacher.

Use your written list of standards during recruiting to illustrate the commitments made by the current teaching staff. As you recruit, discuss the standards with each new candidate. Remind him or her that God sets standards for those who work in His kingdom. You cannot recruit one who does not have a willing spirit, but willing is not quite enough.

DEVELOP LISTS AND RECORD-KEEPING TECHNIQUES

Looking for more people to contact about possible ministry is an ongoing part of recruiting. Make lists of names and develop a record-keeping system that will become the framework for all future recruiting.

Look for: names of those who are not yet involved in any area of ministry

names of people you don't know

Record: name
address
telephone number
Christian commitment
previous areas of ministry
personal interests
professional experience

Names of potential teachers are found in any of the following places. As you look at each of these lists, record as much information about each person as possible.

1. Church membership application cards
The application form for church membership frequently records areas of Christian service and personal interest. Check these forms first as an excellent source of information for recruiting prospects. Talk to your minister about seeing the cards of current members of your church. Look for some people who have taught in the past; they are often willing to become involved again.

2. Adult Sunday school class lists and other Bible study group lists
These sources will include names of people who should be put on your starting list. When you find names of people you don't know, make notes, and then talk to the class or group leader for more information.

3. Outdated committee lists
Many people who have served on short-term committees are willing to

become involved in other ministries. Their willingness to be a part of the previous group is a good reason to contact them for service now. Make a point to contact any who are not involved in another department's ministry.

4. *New converts list*
5. *Potential members list*
6. *Visitors list*

Include as many different groups as possible in your search for names for your file. You may meet those who would like to be involved in ministry but were never approached. Often visitors will continue to attend your church without becoming a part of a smaller group. Your personal contact may be a good step toward a further commitment to Christ and to ministry.

Continue to add the names, addresses, telephone numbers, and experience (professional and volunteer) of as many people as possible to your recruiting file.

Give a copy of your newly compiled list to your education committee, your minister, and other staff members. Ask them to prayerfully consider each person on the list as a teaching candidate, and ask them for information about each person's leadership potential. In addition, take time to get acquainted with these new people, as fellow believers and new friends, not just as potential workers.

As you collect lists of names, you will soon need to organize them in a useful way. Create a file of information, a database on cards or computer, as a tool for your future recruiting. If the church's records are kept on computer, you may be able to sort those records and use them as the basic format of your file. If records are not on the computer, make a card file. Use one card for each adult who is now involved or is a prospect for ministry.

```
Name _____      Area of Service

Address _____      _____

_____      Date Began

Telephone _____      _____

Birthdate _____      Years of Service _____

Background _____

Comments _____

_____

Contact date _____Referred By _____

Result _____      Date _____
```

© 1994 by The Standard Publishing Company. Permission is granted to reproduce this page for ministry purposes only—not for resale.

Decide the most efficient way to organize this card file or computer database. As you talk to people and make contacts, helpful categories will become obvious. Organize your recruiting file as a permanent record as well as a reminder of whom to contact and when. Include the following categories.

Now in Ministry
A. On-going ministry
This includes a card for each one currently teaching, assisting, or serving in some area of ministry within the church or community. Include basic information such as age of class being taught, dates of service, and other interests.
B. Substitutes and short-term or specialized ministries
File those who are actively substituting, or who have volunteered for only a short time, or in a unique capacity. Check this section frequently. Some people listed in this section may be able to move into areas of more active or extensive ministry.

Recruiting Prospects
A. Contact in near future
This category should be divided by dates, perhaps broken down into monthly sections. Include those who are not available now, but have asked that you call them later. Put their names in next month's section. Others in this category include those who have taught in the past but who are now having time off. Put those names in the appropriate section to contact in the future. No one should take six months off and then be forgotten. Organize this file so you will be reminded to make the contact.
B. Contact needed
This is the place for the new names. While you are contacting those you have located on church and class records, their cards would stay in this section during that process. When someone suggests a name to you, add it to this section and then begin to get acquainted as you consider him or her for ministry. This is the catchall part of the file, until more information about a person is available.
C. Not interested in any church ministries
It is to be hoped this section of the file is empty. However, when you have contacts that seem to fit here, spend extra time talking to them about the variety of ministries available. Discuss, for instance, the need for prayer partners for classes or the opportunity to read to shut-ins. When you have done all you can to involve these persons in some ministry, continue to pray for them, but leave additional recruiting efforts to the Lord.
Continue to pray for ideas and ways to find new names and make new contacts. As you talk with those who may be interested in ministry other than education, pass their names to other church leaders, or help them find places of service in other departments. This is what recruiting is all about.

GIVE EFFECTIVE ANNOUNCEMENTS

How many announcements are made for more teachers and there is *no* response? How often does someone publicly ask for people to help in the Sunday school and hears *nothing* from new volunteers?

Much of the time, a general announcement to the congregation seems to be ineffective as a recruiting tool. So why do we keep making announcements?

Public announcements are very useful for letting the church body know what the needs are and what is happening within the congregation. Don't give up on public announcements; they are important. However, they can be more effective in getting a response if you concentrate on timing, tone, and technique.

Watch the Timing

Do present the announcement immediately before you take other recruiting steps such as making phone contacts, sending out a mailing, or setting up an information table. Use the announcement as a jumping-off place for individual contacts.

Don't expect the announcement to do the recruiting. Say something like this:

> I will be calling some new acquaintances this week to talk about what we do in our Christian education classes, especially about the opportunity to be a teacher or leader. Have you thought about how you might fit in? I'd like to include you on my telephone list. Please write your name and telephone number on a card, and put it in the offering basket this morning. Just write on the card "Call me about C. E."

Be sure you call anyone who responds, even if you don't think he or she would be an effective leader. Everyone has a place in the church, and you must respond to any who reach out to you. Your consistency and follow-up will be one of the confidence-building factors that creates a strong relationship between leader and staff.

Don't make a public announcement when many members of the congregation are in the midst of rehearsals for a major musical, convention, or other event. Everyone involved, including family members, will recognize the time commitment already being made and won't wish to take on new responsibility. Time your announcement to coincide with a church-wide education event or between major presentations by other church departments.

Listen to Your Tone

Don't say, "We have struggled along with two teachers for 90 children. Don't you think some of you could find it in your hearts to help us out?" Someone may volunteer out of sympathy for these two teachers, but the motivation wouldn't be right.

An upbeat, optimistic tone helps focus on the "why" of volunteering. Avoid remarks based on guilt, discouragement, or need for sympathy, or those that reflect negatively on present volunteers. Remember, you present the opportunity; the Holy Spirit gives the gifts and does the calling.

Use Creative Techniques

Forty-seven-year-old Cliff was an old-timer in Sunday school, but a first-timer when it came to teaching. Yet his public announcement about Christian education was one of the most effective I've heard:

"I never dreamed what an impact this all would make. I spend one hour a week with some kids and two other teachers, and I've gained so much more than I could possibly give." With tears close to the surface, Cliff told the congregation about his experience as a Sunday school assistant. His suggestion that others get involved and information about whom to contact made much more of an impression than the traditional announcement for more workers.

Use as much variety in your public announcements as possible. Interview teachers and learners of all ages about the benefits of your Christian education program. Have a group of children present a choral reading of a psalm, or a presentation of something they might do in class. Imagine the impact of seven-year-olds, about four feet tall, carrying a nine-foot paper image of Goliath across the platform, stopping to tell the minister about the giant. If you want to recruit creative and challenging people, you need to show that teaching is creative and challenging.

Keep the staff of the education department as visible as possible. Because much of our classroom learning takes place in separate groups in closed classrooms, many people may not realize they should be a part of it. To be effective, use appropriate timing, a joyous tone, and creative technique when you go public with your recruiting.

KNOW WHAT TO DO BEFORE YOU RECRUIT

Consider ten good reasons why someone would want to be a part of the teaching team in your congregation. If you can do that, you'll have no problem recruiting the teachers you need.

Take your time to think about your list of reasons. You need to know why a person would want to volunteer before you talk to anyone about doing so. Here are a few ideas to get you started.

You should be a part of the education department of this church because:

1. This is God's church, and you are God's child. (Read Matthew 28:19, 20.) Remind yourself that Jesus is asking *you* to talk to people about Him. Response to God is what the Christian faith is all about.
2. God has given you specific abilities and gifts. They have not been given for just your benefit, but to help others. (Read Romans 12:4, 5.) There are many ways other than teaching to serve the education department. Being a member of a congregation requires service to others in some way.
3. It provides you with an opportunity to show God that you love Him (1 John 5:1-3).

4. It brings you joy. As you help others understand the character of God and their relationship with Him, you will find yourself overflowing with joy (Psalm 126:1-3).
5. The Holy Spirit provides the energy (Colossians 1:28, 29).
6. Sharing the Gospel is essential to your own spiritual growth (Ephesians 4:12, 13).

These are just a few examples of the spiritual rewards and biblical requirements for us as Christians. There are many more to put on your list. For instance, the support and attitudes of the congregation are important factors in attracting volunteers to Christian education ministries. Are the following statements true of your church or do you need to do some work in one or more of these areas?

1. We recognize the influence and responsibility each staff member has as stated in James 3:1, and are careful before God to maintain high standards. You would be proud to be a part of this team.
2. Joyful, happy, intelligent people are involved in our Sunday school, and it is uplifting to be with them.
3. We recognize that you are a volunteer giving your time; therefore, appreciation is expressed frequently in a variety of ways—by the congregation as well as by the class members and others.
4. We emphasize the value and high priority of studying the Scriptures as the very foundation of our faith. The congregation is kept well informed of the studies and activities of each class. Your contribution to God's church is important.
5. Regular fellowship and staff gatherings reinforce the joy of being in the service of the Lord. Although you may teach students outside your own age group, we are careful to help you avoid feeling isolated or alone.
6. Prayer support is ongoing; a prayer ministry with those in the congregation is a vital part of the education department. The church practices Galatians 6:2.
7. Experienced and mature teachers and pastors are interested in helping you with any problem or concern, either in the classroom or of a personal nature.
8. Appropriate training is provided before you begin any new area of responsibility. Supplies and equipment are available quickly and cheerfully.
9. Each participant makes a commitment for a specific length of time for each responsibility, so the acceptance of a task is not the equivalent of "a life sentence."

If the current teachers and assistants are respected and honored, others will be interested in joining them.

As you evaluate what *is* and look ahead to what *will be*, ask God for an added measure of the Holy Spirit's joy on your teaching staff. It will be catching, and recruiting will be easier. Try it!

WRITE MINISTRY DESCRIPTIONS

"How much time will it take?"

"I'm not really qualified. Do you think I could do it?

"What's involved?"

"I don't think I can teach, but I'm great with crafts."

One of the most important tools for effective recruiting is written ministry descriptions. These brief statements describe what is involved in a specific position or ministry, and include the necessary time commitment and qualifications. Each one should be short enough to fit on a 3" x 5" card.

As you begin recruiting, write ministry descriptions for everything volunteers do or could do in the education department. Make a list of *all* the volunteer possibilities within your congregation, not just those that currently need some help. Talk to the other church leaders and include all the different church ministries—teachers, nursery care-givers, musicians, ushers, telephoners, and visitation team members. If possible, have this list correspond with the interest survey you use (see pages 63 and 64).

You will find many uses for these ministry descriptions. Use them on bulletin boards, as handouts, and in mailings to alert individuals to the many ministry opportunities available within the church body.

In addition to these brief summaries, write more detailed ministry descriptions, and keep them in the appropriate place available for browsing.

Samples

NURSERY ATTENDANT, INFANTS: CARE FOR PHYSICAL AND EMOTIONAL NEEDS OF INFANTS, BIRTH TO ONE YEAR.

TIME COMMITMENT:
1½ HOURS EACH SUNDAY MORNING FOR A THREE-WEEK PERIOD, ONCE EVERY FOUR MONTHS.

QUALIFICATIONS:
LOVE FOR GOD AND LOVE FOR CHILDREN. WILLINGNESS TO BE TRAINED. NO EXPERIENCE NECESSARY.

TEACHER, third grade:	Time commitment:	Qualifications:
Teach God's Word using a printed curriculum of methods and ideas.	Weekly: 1½ hours on Sunday morning and at least 1 hour outside preparation. Monthly: 2 hour staff fellowship.	Love for God, love for children, and a willingness to learn teaching techniques. No experience necessary. Training provided.

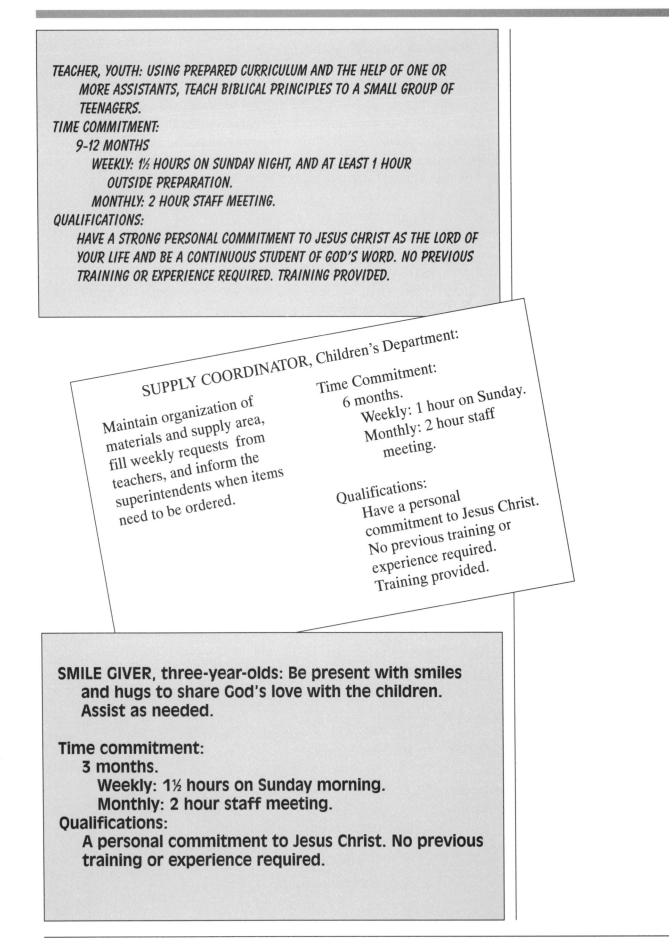

TEACHER, YOUTH: USING PREPARED CURRICULUM AND THE HELP OF ONE OR MORE ASSISTANTS, TEACH BIBLICAL PRINCIPLES TO A SMALL GROUP OF TEENAGERS.

TIME COMMITMENT:

9-12 MONTHS

WEEKLY: 1½ HOURS ON SUNDAY NIGHT, AND AT LEAST 1 HOUR OUTSIDE PREPARATION.

MONTHLY: 2 HOUR STAFF MEETING.

QUALIFICATIONS:

HAVE A STRONG PERSONAL COMMITMENT TO JESUS CHRIST AS THE LORD OF YOUR LIFE AND BE A CONTINUOUS STUDENT OF GOD'S WORD. NO PREVIOUS TRAINING OR EXPERIENCE REQUIRED. TRAINING PROVIDED.

SUPPLY COORDINATOR, Children's Department:

Maintain organization of materials and supply area, fill weekly requests from teachers, and inform the superintendents when items need to be ordered.

Time Commitment:
6 months.
Weekly: 1 hour on Sunday.
Monthly: 2 hour staff meeting.

Qualifications:
Have a personal commitment to Jesus Christ. No previous training or experience required. Training provided.

SMILE GIVER, three-year-olds: Be present with smiles and hugs to share God's love with the children. Assist as needed.

Time commitment:
3 months.
Weekly: 1½ hours on Sunday morning.
Monthly: 2 hour staff meeting.
Qualifications:
A personal commitment to Jesus Christ. No previous training or experience required.

CLASS PARENT, fifth and sixth grades:

Be available for class activities to assist as needed.

Time commitment: 9-12 months. Monthly: 2-3 hours.

Qualifications: A personal commitment to Jesus Christ. No previous training or experience required.

BUS DRIVER: USE THE CHURCH VAN TO DRIVE A GROUP OF PEOPLE TO AND FROM THE CHURCH BUILDING.

TIME COMMITMENT:
1 HOUR BEFORE AND 1 HOUR AFTER THE WEEKLY EVENT YOU CHOOSE (I.E., SUNDAY MORNING OR EVENING, WEDNESDAY EVENING, OR SPECIAL EVENTS).

QUALIFICATIONS:
APPROPRIATE DRIVER'S LICENSE AND PHYSICAL EXAM (ALL COSTS FOR QUALIFYING TO BE PAID BY THE CHURCH).

SUBSTITUTE TEACHER: Be on call to teach a group of children in Children's Church using the packet of materials prepared for class substitutes.

Time commitment:
As needed for six months, 1½ hours weekly.

Qualifications:
A personal commitment to Jesus Christ. Training is provided. Previous experience is preferred.

Section 2
Recruiting Plans

Here are the recruiting ideas you need, ready for immediate use!

Successful recruiting requires a variety of presentations, creative publicity about your Christian education in action, and the use of several techniques for locating and contacting potential teachers. Use Section 2 to help you do just that. These plans are already designed and many items are ready to be photocopied. Each plan begins with an overview to help you select one quickly and easily.

An extended recruiting focus should be used once a year. This plan would include several weeks of exposure to the entire church congregation with posters and photographs, announcements, an information table, and other items all related to the plan's theme.

At other times during the year, recruit with a bulletin board, a flyer, or a brief presentation about Christian education to explain the need for additional teachers.

Section 2 is designed to give your recruiting variety with ease.

"Be sure to wear a flower in your lapel for the next four Sundays."

"Why?"

"I can't tell you. That's part of the plan. Just wear a flower from your garden. We want to create some curiosity for two weeks, so don't tell anyone I asked you to do it or explain what it's all about."

When it is time to recruit some new teachers, go for flowers.

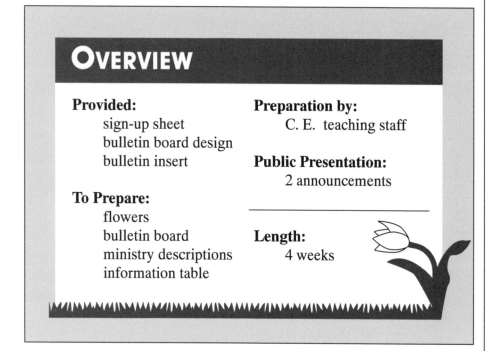

OVERVIEW

Provided:
sign-up sheet
bulletin board design
bulletin insert

To Prepare:
flowers
bulletin board
ministry descriptions
information table

Preparation by:
C. E. teaching staff

Public Presentation:
2 announcements

Length:
4 weeks

Planning

Start this recruiting plan with a meeting or a letter to all the current teachers and staff in the Christian Education Department. Ask all the Christian education workers to wear flowers for the following four Sunday mornings. Offer no explanation. The mystery element will call attention to what you are doing. Purchase carnations or other easily obtainable flowers to have on hand each Sunday for those who may forget or have no flowers available.

Information Table

Set up the information table for the third and fourth Sundays. Decorate this location with flowers. Have as hosts some of the C. E. workers who are excited that God is using the Sunday school to bring about life changes.

Distribute copies of ministry descriptions printed on 3" x 5" cards to provide information about as many opportunities for ministry as possible. Each ministry description should explain the task involved, the time commitment, and qualifications needed (see pages 19–21).

Use the sign-up sheet on page 27 to gather names and telephone numbers of those who want more information. You may wish to give a flower to each one who comes by the information table. Perhaps children or a ladies' group could make flowers for this purpose.

Bulletin board ideas:
- Make a border with colorful floral wrapping paper, wide ribbon, or fabric.
- Mount ministry descriptions onto simple flower shapes cut from colored paper or flower pictures cut from seed catalogs, magazines, or greeting cards.
- Cut grass border from green paper.
- Use stencils to draw letters or purchase a punch-out alphabet set.

Bulletin Board

Ready the bulletin board for the third and fourth Sundays. Choose a central location so that everyone in the congregation can see it. Post ministry descriptions (see pages 19-21) and short stories of those in your church whose lives have been changed through Sunday school. Copy the sign-up sheet on page 27, and post it on the bulletin board.

Bulletin Insert and Announcements

Use the bulletin insert from page 26 to express appreciation to the current staff and to invite others to become involved. Add a list of C. E. workers in the box on side one. Include the church name, address, and telephone number at the bottom of side two. Cut the original in half and photocopy halves back to back. Make enough copies for distribution on the third and fourth Sundays.

Also on the third and fourth Sundays, make announcements about the flowers, and express appreciation for those already making a difference in the Sunday school. Mention the information table and its location, directing people to visit it after church.

For an additional announcement, ask someone from the congregation to explain how Sunday school has made a difference in his or her life and to invite everyone to stop by the information table to find out about making a difference.

side 1

side 2

Follow-up

As soon as possible, contact all those who have expressed an interest on the sign-up sheet. Discuss the opportunities for ministry, time for prayer before decisions are made, and the training and observation time provided. Direct each interested person to others who can answer questions, and give appropriate guidance about a commitment to ministry.

HAVE YOU NOTICED THE FLOWERS?

They are being worn by people who are making a difference! We give thanks to God for the following people who are a part of the Christian education program, sharing God's Word with children, youth, and adults every week. God is using them to make a difference in our community and our world.

We appreciate these leaders
who are committed to ministry to the Lord
and to sharing His love with others.

You Can Make a Difference!
Teach Sunday School!

Do you think something should be done about the declining values in our country?　　YES ☐　　NO ☐

Can we build now weakening adult-child relationships?　　YES ☐　　NO ☐

Do we need to provide a higher quality education?　　YES ☐　　NO ☐

Visit the flower table for more information about how you can make a difference.

Start wearing a FLOWER!

© 1994 by The Standard Publishing Company. Permission is granted to reproduce this page for ministry purposes only—not for resale.

I'll wear a FLOWER

I want to make a difference. Please call me with some more information.

Name	Phone Number

© 1994 by The Standard Publishing Company. Permission is granted to reproduce this page for ministry purposes only—not for resale.

"Kathi has been searching for peace for more than five years. She tried a lot of different things including the New Age philosophy. Recently she made a commitment to Christ, and changes in her life are already obvious. Now with Christ she is conscious not only of His peace but of His supernatural power."

A young woman told this story to her Sunday school class. The story of Kathi's conversion was exciting to them as they shared the joy of a new believer. They studied God's Word every week; once again what they read came alive in a person.

In another classroom three-year-old Kevin looked out the window at the rain splashing on the sidewalk and into the flower bed. He turned to his teacher and said, "Look, God's watering the ground. Isn't God nice?"

This spontaneous response from the heart of a child and Kathi's earnest belief in Jesus are just two illustrations of God's involvement with individuals. They are only part of God's story. Every church, every Sunday school class, and every teacher has a story to tell.

Because the Bible says to talk about what God has done and is doing (Deuteronomy 6:20-25 and Psalm 78:1-8), these stories should be told to everyone in the church. As others share in the joy and excitement of God at work, they will want to become a part.

Have an "I Have a Story to Tell Month." Tell lots of stories and then invite new people to join the storytellers.

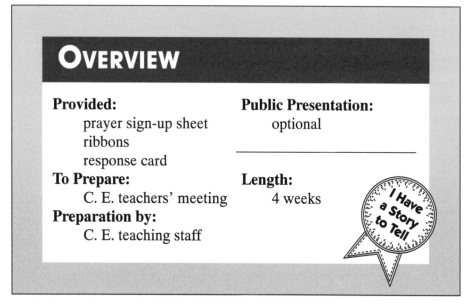

OVERVIEW

Provided:
    prayer sign-up sheet
    ribbons
    response card

To Prepare:
    C. E. teachers' meeting

Preparation by:
    C. E. teaching staff

Public Presentation:
    optional

Length:
    4 weeks

I Have a Story to Tell

Planning

Have a meeting of all current teaching staff, and challenge them to share the stories they live each week. Begin by telling stories from your own experiences. Then ask teachers to recall things that have been happening in their classes: faith-building experiences and thanks to God, searching questions about God's character, or laughs the class has enjoyed.

The stories can come from any source, but the closer to home the better. Remind teachers that each week they are in the midst of people who know God, are obedient to His Word, are living it, and putting it into action every day.

Explain that the teachers are to wear ribbons for four Sundays, and when asked about it, they can respond with one of "God's stories." Be sure that everyone has at least one story he or she would like to tell, regardless of the age level taught. Help everyone on the teaching staff—from nursery workers and shy assistants to experienced, gregarious teachers—to be comfortable with sharing at least a sentence about God at work in His church.

Spend time in prayer together, asking God to help you to spread the encouragement and excitement of being involved in His story each week. Ask for wisdom about sharing personal stories. Use the Prayer Commitment Sign-up on page 31 and ask each teacher to make a commitment to daily prayer throughout "I Have a Story to Tell Month."

Ribbons

Use the patterns on page 30 to photocopy and cut out enough ribbons for all the C. E. teaching staff. These can be worn throughout the month, with the teachers ready to tell a story when asked about the ribbons.

Response Card

Add your church name, address, and telephone number to the bottom of the response card (see page 30) before photocopying. Also add instructions to the bottom of the card such as:

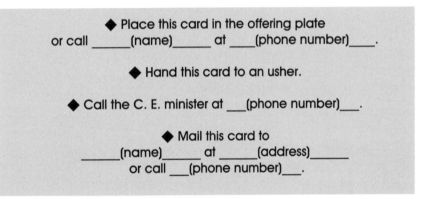

Put copies of the response card in the pew rack or bulletins and in the church lobby. Find other ways to distribute them if you choose not to make a public announcement.

Optional Announcements

At the end of a month of ribbon-wearing and storytelling, give a public announcement or write one for the church bulletin. Ask people to become a part of the stories they have been hearing. Distribute the response card with instructions about how to return it for more information.

Follow-up

Within a few days, contact all those who have returned a response card. Discuss with each one the opportunities currently available for ministry, and suggest that time be spent in prayer before any decisions are made. Talk about preparation and training plans that can be used. When appropriate, direct the interested persons to others who can answer questions and encourage a commitment to ministry.

Ribbons

Directions:

Photocopy onto cardstock paper and cut out these badges. Use straight pins to attach them to clothing. Or cut cloth ribbon to the same size and write these words on them. Actual ribbon could also be attached to the bottom of the round badge replacing the paper ribbon.

Response Card

Directions:

Photocopy four cards onto 8 ½" x 11" cardstock paper and cut apart.

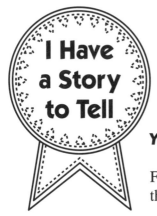

LIVING AND TELLING GOD'S STORIES!

Have you heard one of God's stories from a Sunday school teacher?

You can be a part of a new story!

For more information about how you can join the teaching staff, fill in the information below.

_____

Name   Phone Number

© 1994 by The Standard Publishing Company. Permission is granted to reproduce this page for ministry purposes only—not for resale.

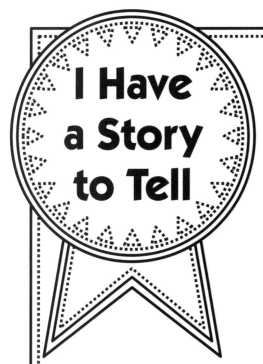

I Have a Story to Tell

Prayer Commitment Sign-up

I will pray during "I Have A Story to Tell Month" for God to use His stories to call teachers and assistants.

Name

© 1994 by The Standard Publishing Company. Permission is granted to reproduce this page for ministry purposes only—not for resale.

"Do Sunday school teachers live at church? Where do they sleep?"

"Sunday school teachers have to know lots of things. Have you heard about those guys that go out in a sailboat?"

"Dear minister, I like my Sunday school teacher. He plays Bible baseball with us and took us skating. Are there more people like him for my sister's class? Love, Brad."

If you give the children an opportunity to express to the congregation what they think about Sunday school teachers, you can do some valuable recruiting.

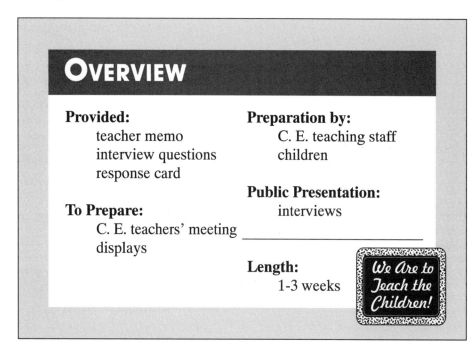

OVERVIEW

Provided:
teacher memo
interview questions
response card

To Prepare:
C. E. teachers' meeting
displays

Preparation by:
C. E. teaching staff
children

Public Presentation:
interviews

_____

Length:
1-3 weeks

We Are to Teach the Children!

Planning

Discuss these plans with the current teaching staff in the children's department, especially those with classes of children in kindergarten through sixth grade. Explain that you would like the children to communicate to the congregation what they think a Sunday school teacher is, what kind of a person makes a good teacher, and why teachers and assistants are important. Some Sunday school class time can be used for the children to write letters or sentences and draw pictures. Give the teachers detailed instructions about what you need and when, and provide extra help as needed. A reproducible, explanation letter to teachers is provided on page 34. Print it on church stationary.

Plan a Sunday when it would be appropriate to present a short feature in the worship service. Then arrange for the children's letters and essays to be written several weeks in advance to allow for printing and preparation.

Children's Letters, Sentences, and Pictures

Children will add variety to your recruiting program, as well as humor and personality. As an important part of your congregation, they need the opportunity to share their thoughts about Sunday school and teachers. Further, they can effectively recruit new adults into your education department.

You will want to use the children's projects in several ways, making sure you use *all* of them. Feature the children's work on bulletin boards, in adult classrooms, hallways, the lobby, and other public locations around your church. Some of the letters can be printed in the bulletin, a mailer, on a handout placed in the lobby, or read during a class or service.

Interviews

Before the designated Sunday(s), arrange for at least two children to conduct two separate interviews during the worship service, one with a minister and one with a teacher. Meet with the children ahead of time and discuss the questions to be asked. Have each child write out the questions and give specific pointers about conducting an interview. Suggest that each interview end with a question and answer about how others can get involved in teaching.

At another time, have an adult interview several children from different classes. Talk about what kind of person they think a teacher should be.

Here are some possible interview questions.

Child to Adult:
1. What did you do in Sunday school when you were my age?
2. What kind of teachers did they have back then?
3. How does someone become a Sunday school teacher?

Adult to Child:
1. What advice would you give a new Sunday school teacher?
2. Do you think it is hard to be a teacher? Why, or why not?
3. Will you be a teacher for children when you grow up?
4. What do you have to do to become a Sunday school teacher?

Response Card

front

back

Follow-up

Cut page 35 in half and photocopy halves back to back, printing two response cards at a time. Prior to printing add your church name, address, telephone number, and instructions for returning the card to the back.

After each public interview let some children distribute the response cards among the congregation and collect them in the same service. Have additional response cards attached to the displays of art and written work.

As soon as possible, contact all those who have expressed an interest on a response card. Discuss the opportunities for ministry, setting aside time for prayer before decisions are made, and the training and observation time provided. Direct each interested person to others who can answer questions and give appropriate guidance about a commitment to ministry.

Dear teachers,

Please spend a few minutes with your class next Sunday talking about the following subjects. You may want to write these questions on the chalkboard. Feel free to add your own questions, or use fewer if your students are very young.

- What is Sunday school?
- Why do you come to Sunday school?
- What is the job of a Sunday school teacher?
- What kind of person makes the best teacher?
- Does a teacher ever need someone to help him? Why?

After discussion, ask children to write either a letter to the minister or a few sentences about a Sunday school teacher. As time permits, let them illustrate what they have written. We will be using *all* of these letters, sentences, and pictures during the next few weeks in different ways.

Thanks!

© 1994 by The Standard Publishing Company. Permission is granted to reproduce this page for ministry purposes only—not for resale.

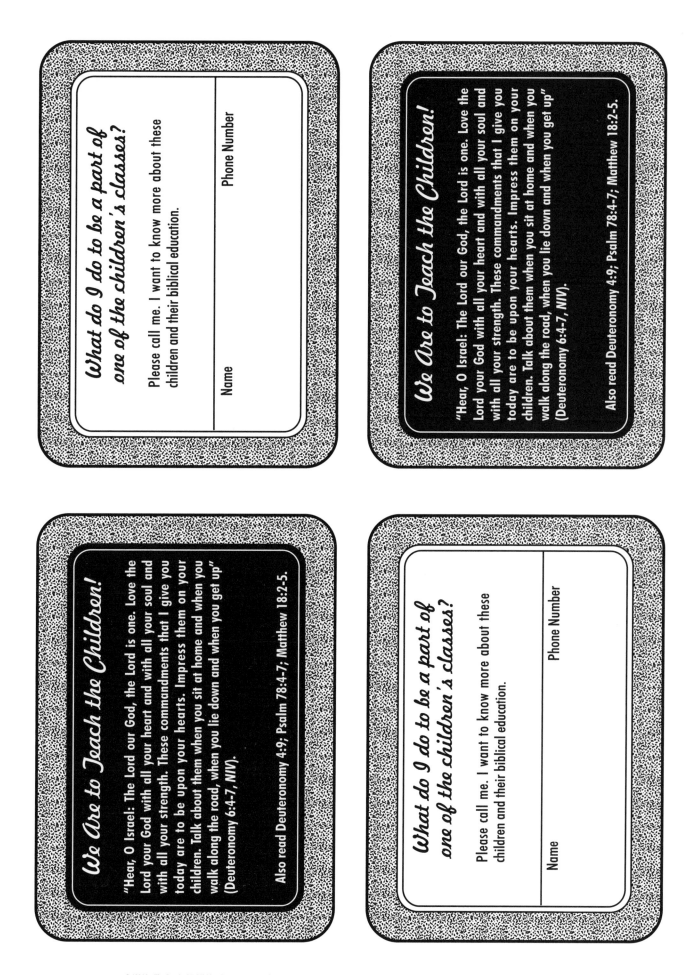

What do I do to be a part of one of the children's classes?

Please call me. I want to know more about these children and their biblical education.

Name _____

Phone Number _____

We Are to Teach the Children!

"Hear, O Israel: The Lord our God, the Lord is one. Love the Lord your God with all your heart and with all your soul and with all your strength. These commandments that I give you today are to be upon your hearts. Impress them on your children. Talk about them when you sit at home and when you walk along the road, when you lie down and when you get up" (Deuteronomy 6:4-7, NIV).

Also read Deuteronomy 4:9; Psalm 78:4-7; Matthew 18:2-5.

We Are to Teach the Children!

"Hear, O Israel: The Lord our God, the Lord is one. Love the Lord your God with all your heart and with all your soul and with all your strength. These commandments that I give you today are to be upon your hearts. Impress them on your children. Talk about them when you sit at home and when you walk along the road, when you lie down and when you get up" (Deuteronomy 6:4-7, NIV).

Also read Deuteronomy 4:9; Psalm 78:4-7; Matthew 18:2-5.

What do I do to be a part of one of the children's classes?

Please call me. I want to know more about these children and their biblical education.

Name _____

Phone Number _____

© 1994 by The Standard Publishing Company. Permission is granted to reproduce this page for ministry purposes only—not for resale.

"Speaking the truth in love, we will in all things grow up into him who is the Head, that is, Christ. From him the whole body, joined and held together by every supporting ligament, grows and builds itself up in love, as each part does its work" (Ephesians 4:15, 16).

We are all a part of God's body, the church, each contributing to the strength of another, influencing, encouraging, and doing the work of the ministry. Help others understand their responsibilities to be a part of this team.

OVERVIEW

Provided:
  poster
  sign-up sheet
  instruction card tent
  button

To Prepare:
  information table
  ministry descriptions
  photography

Preparation by:
  C. E. committee

Public Presentation:
  optional

Length:
  3 weeks

Planning

Set aside several Sundays for a recruiting focus. Appoint a committee made up of one person from each class or group in the education department (i.e., adult classes, youth department, boys and girls club programs, children's Sunday school department, children's church). Have this committee write ministry descriptions (see pages 19-21) and prepare needed materials. Use an information table to provide visual, oral, and written information about Christian education ministries. Distribute buttons to the C. E. workers to wear during these weeks. You may also wish to use bulletin notices, pulpit announcements, and letters to parents to direct the congregation's attention to your information table and the ministry descriptions found there.

Poster and Information table

Sign-up Sheet

Ministry Descriptions and Instruction Tent Card

Buttons

Photography

Follow-up

Photocopy the poster on page 39. Place multiple copies around the church facilities to promote the event.

Set up an information table for about three weeks in a central location to be the focal point for meeting potential volunteers and sharing the excitement of being involved in God's church.

Decorate with foil stars and crepe paper or ribbon to carry out the poster theme. Reproduce the poster words onto large poster board and display above the table. Place several people at this table before and after each worship service to answer questions and encourage people to use the sign-up sheet.

Use the sign-up sheet on page 40 for those people who would like information about C. E. involvement. Instruct your teaching staff to take the initiative to ask people if they are currently involved, and if they are willing to receive a phone call with more information. Most importantly, ask the table hosts to stress that a name and phone number on the sign-up sheet does not mean a commitment of any kind.

Make multiple copies of any ministry descriptions (see pages 19-21), and distribute these to those visiting the information table. Offer as many descriptions of nonteaching ministries as possible to provide a variety of ways to serve God. Use the instruction tent card on page 38. You may also want to have more detailed ministry descriptions printed and kept in a binder at the table, available for browsing.

Make buttons using the pattern on page 38. Ask the teachers to wear these buttons and also ask them to direct people to the information table.

Illustrate your Christian education in action with a continuous slide show set up on or near the information table. Include a snapshot poster, video, projects, or classroom displays as visual tools. Be sure all classes and groups are represented, and change the presentation each week. This way people will return to the table to be sure they have seen everyone (especially their own children!).

It is extremely important that you call all who sign-up for more information and discuss interests and answer questions. With God's help, do everything you can to ensure that all become involved in some kind of ministry, as abilities and gifts allow.

Button

I'm a
part
of the
team!

Ephesians 4:16

Directions:

Photocopy buttons onto colored paper. Add foil star stickers if desired. (Half-inch star stickers are available from Standard Publishing.) Attach to clothing with a straight pin.

(This button can be used with the Badge-A-Minit button assembly press.)

Instruction Tent Card

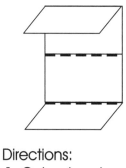

Directions:
1. Cut out rectangle.
2. Fold on broken lines.
3. Staple or tape the overlapped end sections.

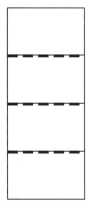

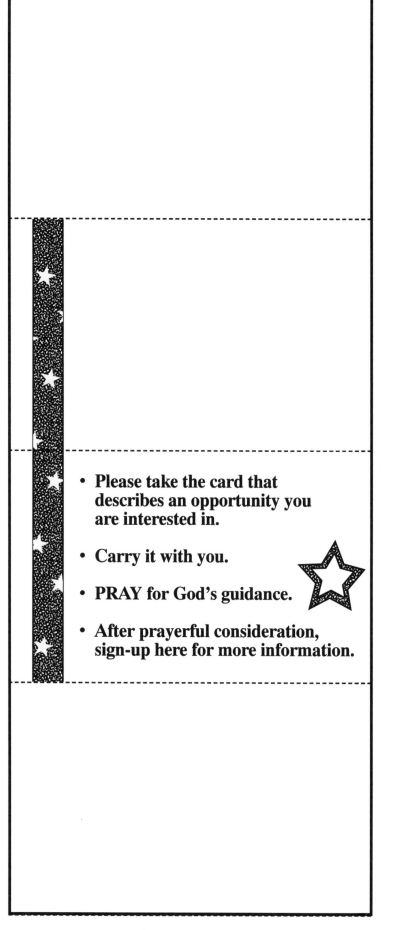

- **Please take the card that describes an opportunity you are interested in.**

- **Carry it with you.**

- **PRAY for God's guidance.**

- **After prayerful consideration, sign-up here for more information.**

© 1994 by The Standard Publishing Company. Permission is granted to reproduce this page for ministry purposes only—not for resale.

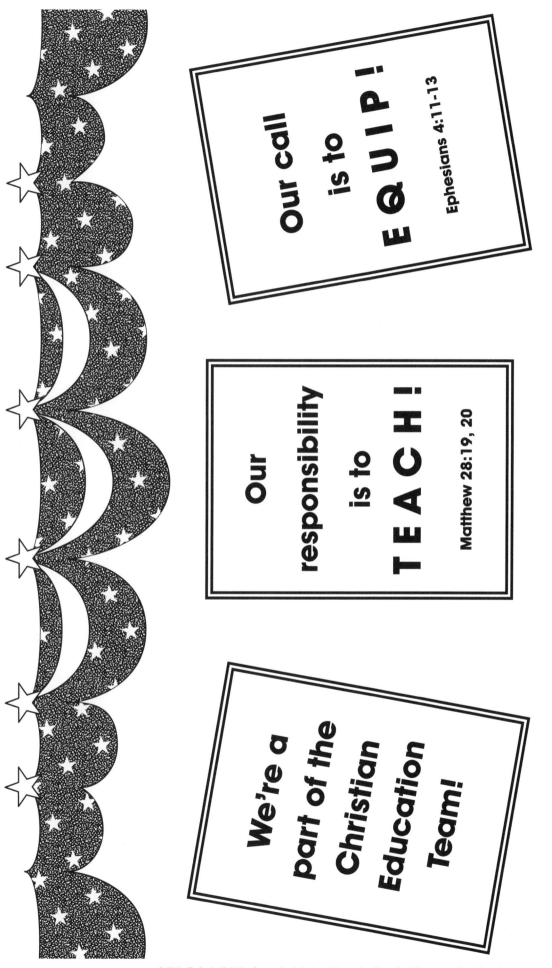

Our call is to **EQUIP!**

Ephesians 4:11-13

Our responsibility is to **TEACH!**

Matthew 28:19, 20

We're a part of the Christian Education Team!

© 1994 by The Standard Publishing Company. Permission is granted to reproduce this page for ministry purposes only—not for resale.

What will you do to serve your Lord?

Sign here for more information.

Name   **Telephone**

Be a part of God's team!
Ephesians 4:16

© 1994 by The Standard Publishing Company. Permission is granted to reproduce this page for ministry purposes only—not for resale.

SHARE PREVIEWS AND APPRECIATION

"I didn't grow up in Sunday school. I'm not even sure what goes on in some of the classes. I don't know whether I'd like to be a teacher or not."

"I used to be good at working with teenagers, but I haven't done it for a while. Everyone says that kids are different these days. I don't know if I'd fit."

"I like kids, but we don't have any children of our own. Do you really think I'd know what to do? Some children ask very strange questions, and I just feel inexperienced."

Do these comments sound familiar? Do you have people in your church who are great prospects for teachers, but who aren't ready to give you a "Yes" to the "Will you?" question?

Try this approach: Set up a "Preview and Appreciation Month" and end it with an all-church dessert celebration to honor current teachers.

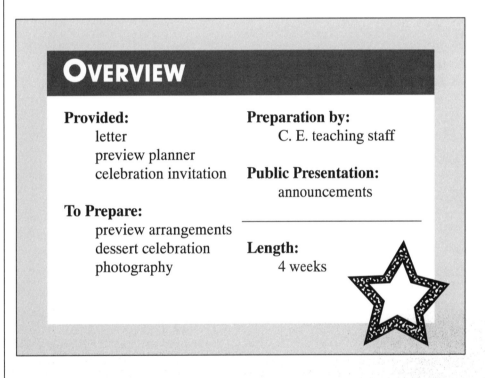

OVERVIEW

Provided:
    letter
    preview planner
    celebration invitation

To Prepare:
    preview arrangements
    dessert celebration
    photography

Preparation by:
    C. E. teaching staff

Public Presentation:
    announcements

Length:
    4 weeks

Planning

Begin by talking to your teaching staff about potential teachers previewing classes in session. Explain that this preview session is to expose new people to the Sunday school and its benefits to different age students. Each prospective teacher would be invited to preview up to three classes of different age levels such as four-year-olds, third grade, and high school. This may be especially helpful to those who have never taught.

Ask all of your current teachers to consider inviting preview visitors to attend their classes, but only schedule with those who are comfortable with the concept. Take the time to discuss how to make an adult visitor feel at home in the classroom such as inviting the guest to help a child with a specific task, asking students to include the visitor in some activity, or asking the visitor to assist in some way. At this point do not have a visitor actually lead the class; he or she is to be an observer only.

Send a letter to all the adults and older teenagers who are not currently involved in some area of ministry. Copy the letter on page 43, using church stationary. You may also want to put a notice in the bulletin and church mailer.

Follow up each response of interest and make specific arrangements for each previewer to visit several classes, one each week, so he or she can stay for the full class time. Use the form on page 44 as you also make arrangements with each teacher whose class will be previewed.

During "Preview and Appreciation Month," have several people take slides or make video recordings of all classes in all departments. Include close-ups of teachers and activities to present an accurate representation of Christian education in action.

At the end of the month have an all-church dessert celebration to honor your teachers. Send special invitations to the previewers so they can see and hear about other teachers and classes. Also send invitations to all C. E. workers to be honored. Photocopy the invitation on page 45. Fold invitations in thirds and seal with gummed stars or stickers. Address the backs.

Celebrate by presenting the slide show or video. Include a special prayer of thanksgiving for the gift of teachers God has given to your church.

After each classroom visit, ask the previewer, "What did you enjoy about the class you visited? What did you notice about this age student and his responses in a discussion?" Do not ask about the visitor's interest in teaching until he or she has previewed all classes you scheduled.

At the end of "Preview and Appreciation Month," contact each one who has participated. Send thank-you letters to teachers who were involved as a part of the preview. Talk to those who previewed classes and ask them to prayerfully consider becoming involved in some area of the teaching ministry.

Letter or Bulletin Notice

Preview Planner

Photography

Dessert Celebration

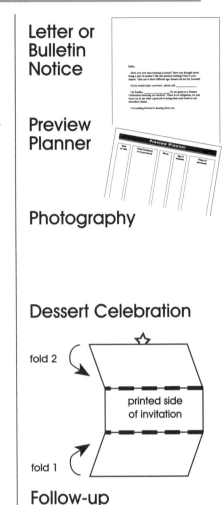

Follow-up

Hello,

Have you ever seen learning in action? Have you thought about being a part of another's life and spiritual training? Here's your chance. Visit one to three different age classes and see for yourself.

If you would enjoy a preview, please call _____.

On Sunday, _____, be our guest at a Dessert Celebration honoring our teachers! There is no obligation; we just want you to see what a great job is being done each week in our education classes.

I'm looking forward to hearing from you.

© 1994 by The Standard Publishing Company. Permission is granted to reproduce this page for ministry purposes only—not for resale.

Preview Planner

Date of visit	Class/Teacher(s) to be previewed	Room	Age of students	Name of previewer

© 1994 by The Standard Publishing Company. Permission is granted to reproduce this page for ministry purposes only—not for resale.

YOU ARE INVITED

Come Celebrate!

You are invited to come and honor the gifts of our Christian education team.

☆☆☆☆☆☆☆☆ Celebrate with us! ☆☆☆☆☆☆☆☆

☆ **Date**   ☆ **Time**

☆ **Place**

© 1994 by The Standard Publishing Company. Permission is granted to reproduce this page for ministry purposes only—not for resale.

At 46, Cliff was a new teacher's assistant in our Sunday school. After a few weeks, he was surprised at what he had learned.

"It is an honor to be in the class with those second graders," he said. "To think that God lets me teach those kids. It's a privilege I wish I had taken advantage of a long time ago. I had no idea teaching was so rewarding."

Cliff isn't the only one who missed the excitement, rewards, challenges, and honor that come from being a part of Sunday school. It is often hard to comprehend that God would choose us, in our imperfection, to teach about His love and His perfection. Yet God has honored us in this way, and He gives us the wisdom and ability to do it.

Recruit some new teachers and assistants by letting your church's congregation know about the honor of their service to God. Ask people to join "God's Honored Roll."

OVERVIEW

Provided:
   name tag
   bookmark
   poster

To Prepare:
   locate speakers

Preparation by:
   C. E. leader
   3 adults

Public Presentation:
   testamonials

_____

Length:
   3 weeks

Planning

Check your church calendar and select two or three Sundays appropriate for a recruiting emphasis. Use bookmarks and name tags to emphasize to the congregation the honor of being in ministry to the Lord. Ask each C. E. worker to wear a name tag each week. After the Sunday when the bookmarks are distributed, put some in the pew racks as an ongoing recruiting tool.

Name Tags

Use the pattern on page 48 to make enough name tags for each C. E. worker. Distribute name tags early the first Sunday morning and ask that teachers, assistants, and others in the educational ministries wear them at all services for the next three weeks.

Bookmarks

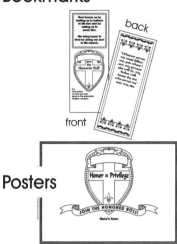

The bookmarks are to be an ongoing recruiting reminder. They provide information as to how to become involved, what contacts to make, or where to go for more information.

Distribute the bookmarks among the congregation on the last Sunday of this honor emphasis. That week's speaker should explain its use and how one can join the "Honored Role" of teachers.

Make the two-sided bookmarks using the pattern on page 48. Add your church name, address, and telephone number to the back and contact information to the front.

Posters

Photocopy multiple copies of the poster on page 49. Include on each poster the names and telephone numbers of persons to contact for more information.

Speakers

An excited Sunday school teacher is one of the best recruiting tools. For each Sunday of this emphasis, ask a teacher or assistant like Cliff to speak briefly to the congregation about the honor of serving God. Ask the speakers to talk about their classroom experiences and to discuss honor as a privilege.

Ask them also to discuss the possibility of everyone being involved in some way, not just in the teaching area.

Follow-up

Be sure to contact all those who have expressed an interest for more information. Talk about giving time to prayer before any decisions are made. Discuss the current opportunities for ministry and the training and observation time provided.

Bookmarks

Directions:
Photocopy four two-sided bookmarks onto 8½" x11" cardstock paper and cut apart.

Name Tag

Directions:
Photocopy onto colored paper and cut out. Write name across the top. Attach to clothing with a straight pin.

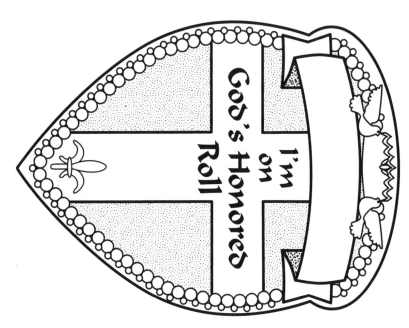

discard

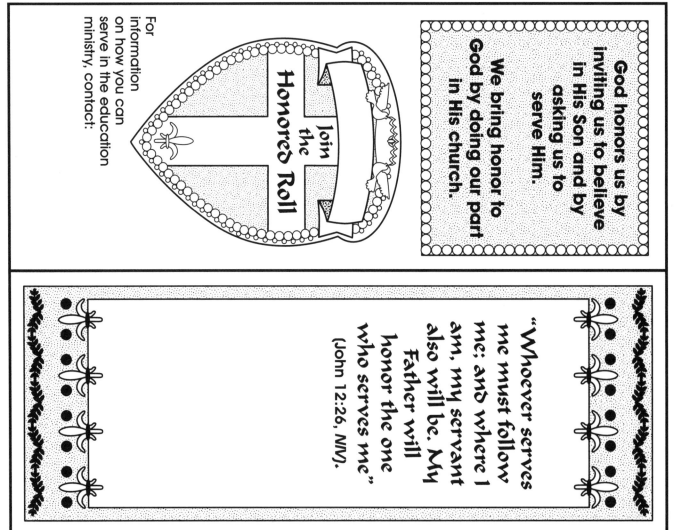

front

back

God honors us by inviting us to believe in His Son and by asking us to serve Him.

We bring honor to God by doing our part in His church.

Join the Honored Roll

For information on how you can serve in the education ministry, contact:

"Whoever serves me must follow me; and where I am, my servant also will be. My Father will honor the one who serves me" (John 12:26, NIV).

I'm on God's Honored Roll

© 1994 by The Standard Publishing Company. Permission is granted to reproduce this page for ministry purposes only—not for resale.

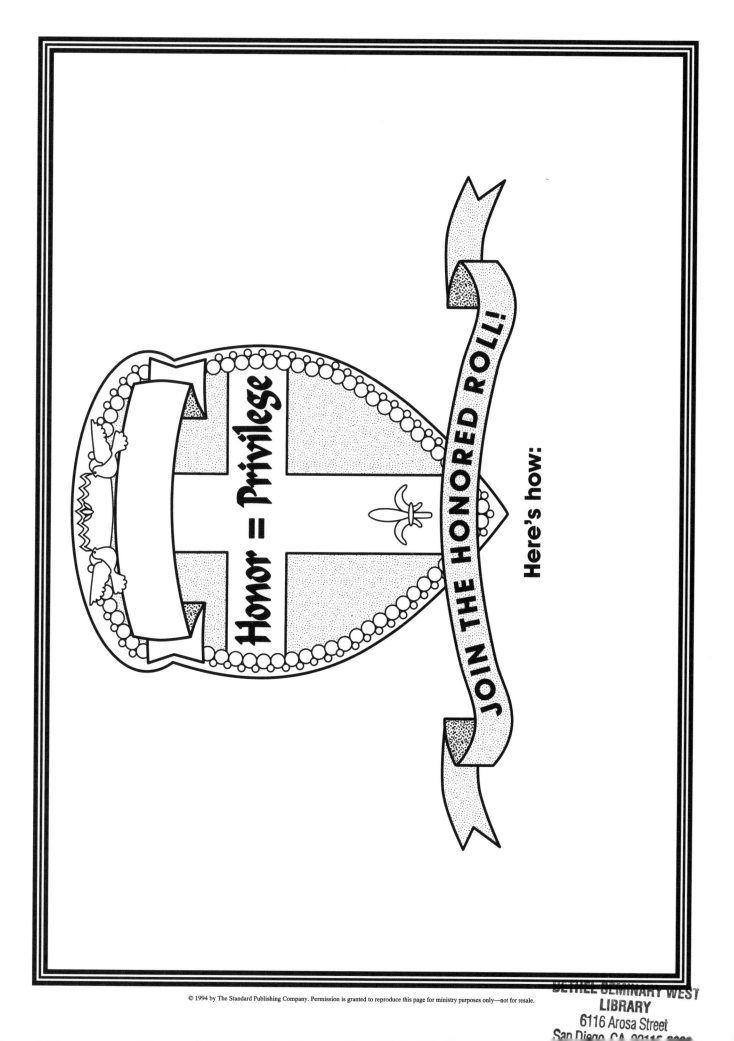

© 1994 by The Standard Publishing Company. Permission is granted to reproduce this page for ministry purposes only—not for resale.

BETHEL SEMINARY WEST
LIBRARY
6116 Arosa Street
San Diego, CA 92115

"I can't seem to get anyone to teach in this church. Is it just us, or does everyone have this problem?" As the Sunday school superintendent, I was expressing my frustrations to a leader in a neighboring church.

"I've talked to many other church leaders. I think it is harder to get volunteers now than it was a few years ago. People seem to be busier or something," Susan replied, comforting me.

"What can we do? We can't just shut down the Sunday school!"

"We can always go to top management. Have you tried that?"

"You mean . . . ?"

"Yes. I mean go to the One whose church this really is. Talk to Him about your recruiting frustrations and get His suggestions."

I followed Susan's advice and found out once again that God does care about His church and who teaches in it. However, He reminded me that I had put the cart before the horse. I was trying to find willing teachers before I asked for the Holy Spirit's guidance; I was approaching people before they were ready to listen. The Holy Spirit's role is to prepare hearts for service, but I was plunging ahead without that assistance. No wonder I was frustrated. Now I know the *first* step of recruiting must be *prayer*.

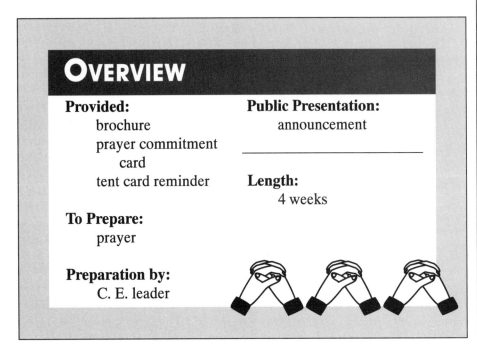

OVERVIEW

Provided:
brochure
prayer commitment card
tent card reminder

To Prepare:
prayer

Preparation by:
C. E. leader

Public Presentation:
announcement

_____

Length:
4 weeks

Planning

Begin your recruiting plans with prayer before you do anything else. Then share the privilege and responsibility of prayer with the congregation by using the brochure and commitment card. Help everyone be a part of this responsibility.

Brochure

The prayer brochure (see pages 53 and 54) includes the W's of Prayer: why, when, and who. Use it to emphasize that our part of recruitment is primarily prayer.

Add your church name, address, and telephone number to the back of the brochure. Photocopy the two-sided brochure and fold in half.

Prayer Commitment Card and Tent Card

Include a commitment card (see below) in the brochure. Ask that the YES! box be checked and the card put in the offering plate or given to an usher. Since this commitment is between the individual and God, a name on the card is optional. However, each person is asked to turn in a card to encourage us as we know that God's people are praying for new teachers.

Also include a tent card reminder (see page 52). Tent cards should be taken home and displayed in a prominent place as a reminder of this commitment.

Announcement

Introduce the brochure and commitment card with an announcement to the congregation. Read Matthew 9:35-38 and explain the need for additional teachers and assistants. Talk about our responsibility to pray that God will fill this need and the interdependence of God's church from ministry to ministry.

Follow-up

Write a bulletin announcement to thank the people in the congregation for their prayers for the Christian Education Department. Tell about the new contacts that have been made and how many people were praying during this month.

Directions:
   Photocopy six cards onto 8½" x 11" cardstock paper and cut apart.

discard

Prayer Commitment Card

❑ YES! I'll join you in prayer every day this month. I'll ask God to call more teachers to help with our Christian education, as written in Matthew 9:35-38.

© 1994 by The Standard Publishing Company. Permission is granted to reproduce this page for ministry purposes only—not for resale.

Tent Card Reminder

Directions:
Photocopy two tent cards onto 8½" x 11" paper and cut apart.

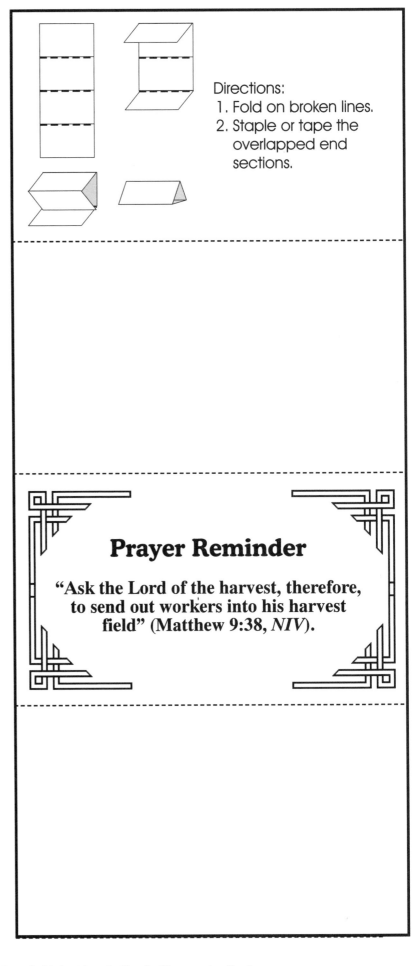

Directions:
1. Fold on broken lines.
2. Staple or tape the overlapped end sections.

Prayer Reminder

"Ask the Lord of the harvest, therefore, to send out workers into his harvest field" (Matthew 9:38, *NIV*).

© 1994 by The Standard Publishing Company. Permission is granted to reproduce this page for ministry purposes only—not for resale.

The W's of Prayer

Why, When, & Who

Who should pray?

The church, as designed by God, is a group of people interrelated and dependent on each other. We have *all* been instructed to pray, and to pray for each other. (See Luke 18:1; Acts 1:14; 1 Corinthians 12:27; Colossians 4:2.)

The education department includes all age levels and wants to include you! The ministerial and educational leader are not the only ones with the responsibility to pray.

Please join us every day for the next four weeks. Read Matthew 9:35-38 and ask God to send new teachers to His learners.

© 1994 by The Standard Publishing Company. Permission is granted to reproduce this page for ministry purposes only—but not for resale.

WHY pray?

Jesus gave us instructions about prayer. Paul, Timothy, and others in Scripture tell us why we should be praying for the recruiting process in our church.

The harvest is plentiful but the workers are few. Ask the Lord of the harvest, therefore, to send out workers into his harvest field (Matthew 9:37, 38, *NIV*).

If you believe, you will receive whatever you ask for in prayer (Matthew 21:22, *NIV*).

God is vitally interested in individuals knowing about Him and committing their lives to Him, but He chose to use people as the method of reaching these individuals.

I urge, then, first of all, that requests, prayers, intercession and thanksgiving be made for everyone . . . . This is good, and pleases God our Savior, who wants all men to be saved and to come to a knowledge of the truth (1 Timothy 2:1-4, *NIV*).

And how can they hear without someone preaching to them? (Romans 10:14, *NIV*).

Praying for new teachers keeps us in constant touch with the One they will be teaching about. Prayer helps us to realize that God is even more concerned than we are.

Pray WHEN?

Scripture reminds us that all believers are to be in prayer *continually* (1 Thessalonians 5:17). Especially before anyone is considered for a position of responsibility in God's church, prayer is essential.

WHAT DO YOU THINK? OPINION POLL

What do the people in your church think about Sunday school teachers and teaching? Is teaching a thankless, unrewarding task to them? Do we really need teachers, or can people learn God's Word another way?

If you don't know what the people in your church are thinking, ask! The answers could help in your recruiting. Most of the people around you have strong opinions about things, but they may not speak up unless you ask for a response. Many won't bother with questionnaires, and few of us will write a letter or give a speech. Here's a way to help people express themselves, even anonymously if they prefer.

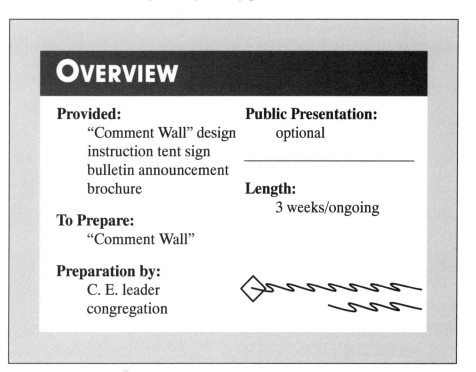

OVERVIEW

Provided:
"Comment Wall" design
instruction tent sign
bulletin announcement
brochure

To Prepare:
"Comment Wall"

Preparation by:
C. E. leader
congregation

Public Presentation:
optional

Length:
3 weeks/ongoing

Select a location in a heavily traveled area of your church such as the lobby or fellowship area. Set up a large "Comment Wall" on a bulletin board or large poster board that people can write on as they walk by. Keep this wall up for three weeks.

Place pens and markers near the "Comment Wall" and display the instruction tent sign on page 56. To stimulate ideas and encourage others to participate, you may want to ask a few people to write on each section before you display the "Comment Wall."

"Comment Wall"

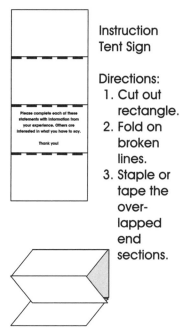

Instruction Tent Sign

Directions:
1. Cut out rectangle.
2. Fold on broken lines.
3. Staple or tape the over-lapped end sections.

Please complete each of these statements with information from your experience. Others are interested in what you have to say.

Thank you!

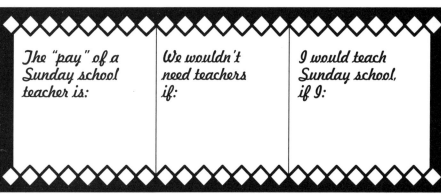

The "pay" of a Sunday school teacher is:

We wouldn't need teachers if:

I would teach Sunday school, if I:

Call attention to the "Comment Wall" each week with a brief announcement or use a bulletin notice such as this:

> What do you think about Sunday school teaching and teachers? Many of you have been teachers during your years of serving Christ. Here's a chance to express your opinion. Visit the "Comment Wall" in the fellowship hall. Read the statements and write your own comments. By letting others know your attitudes, you will help make a difference.

The recruiting value of this interesting project emerges after the "Comment Wall" is taken down. Although some have already read others' comments, continue to use the material in the months to come. Start by making a copy of the quotes. Note things that were repeated more than once. Look for patterns. If quotes are signed, go to those individuals and ask for more information about what they wrote.

Devise different ways to present the information throughout the year. For example, consider the comments about the "pay" of a teacher. Some quotes may be appropriate to print in your church's newsletter.

Prepare a brochure using page 57. Insert your church's name, address, and telephone number in the rectangle, and copy as many brochures as needed. Copy some quotes from the "Comment Wall" on the opposite side to make a two-sided brochure. Fold into thirds.

Look seriously at the comments about why people do not teach Sunday school. What changes can you make in scheduling and training that can help overcome some of these objections?

If you receive a strong response confirming Sunday school teachers, use this in your contacts and announcements. If the comments in the middle portion of the wall were primarily against having Sunday school teachers, talk to your minister and church leaders, and then publicly discuss some of the stated opinions.

Listen to the congregation. Give them the opportunity to tell each other what they think about teachers and teaching. Use their words to encourage new Sunday school teachers to earn the "pay" that is a part of giving. Help the new people in your church understand that teaching is God's design, and they can be a part of it.

Bulletin Announcements

Follow-up

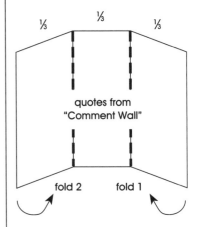

folding of brochure

⅓   ⅓   ⅓

quotes from "Comment Wall"

fold 2   fold 1

Instruction Tent Card

When photocopying, enlarge by at least 150%.

© 1994 by The Standard Publishing Company. Permission is granted to reproduce this page for ministry purposes only—not for resale.

Please complete each of these statements with information from your experience. Others are interested in what you have to say.

Thank you!

What is a Teacher?

"He came to Jesus at night and said, 'Rabbi, we know you are a teacher who has come from God. For no one could perform the miraculous signs you are doing if God were not with him'" (John 3:2, *NIV*).

GOD IS WITH US; WE ARE HIS TEACHERS.

"It was he who gave some to be . . . teachers, to prepare God's people for works of service, so that the body of Christ may be built up until we all reach unity in the faith and in the knowledge of the Son of God and become mature, attaining to the whole measure of the fullness of Christ" (Ephesians 4:11-13, *NIV*).

© 1994 by The Standard Publishing Company. Permission is granted to reproduce this page for ministry purposes only—not for resale.

Have you noticed that teachers often learn more than the students? Somehow this doesn't seem quite right. Isn't the point of Christian education that students do the learning? Teachers have many advantages as teachers. Talk about the personal benefits we have as leaders, and recruit new ones when they find out what happens when a person shares Jesus Christ with others.

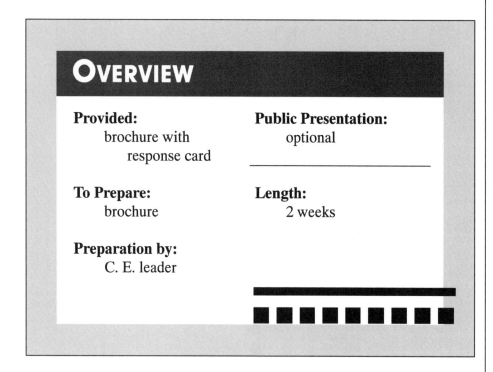

OVERVIEW

Provided:
brochure with
response card

Public Presentation:
optional

To Prepare:
brochure

Length:
2 weeks

Preparation by:
C. E. leader

Use the brochure on pages 59 and 60 to distribute among the congregation or send through the mail. Add your church name, address, and telephone number to the back.

Included in the brochure is a tear-off card requesting more information. Insert directions at the bottom for returning the card. Copy the two-sided brochure and fold each side in to meet in the center.

Ask God for guidance as you help His people find places of service in His church. Follow up every response card and prayerfully discuss the opportunity for involvement with each person. God's Word has many promises of personal blessing. This recruiting tool mentions only a few of the rewards of a committed, giving life. The Christian Education Department provides a wonderful way to be part of this blessing.

Brochure

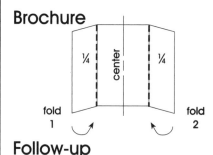

Follow-up

CHRISTIAN EDUCATION

Why be a student of God's Word? Scripture is exciting because of its application to people of every age and ability. Life-long study of the Bible is continually enriching and new. Consider the advantages Paul describes:

Study to show thyself approved unto God, a workman that needeth not to be ashamed, rightly dividing the word of truth (2 Timothy 2:15, *KJV*).

All Scripture is God-breathed and is useful for teaching, rebuking, correcting and training in righteousness, so that the man of God may be thoroughly equipped for every good work (2 Timothy 3:16, 17, *NIV*).

A student of God's Word continues to enjoy the benefits of spiritual growth and a close relationship with God. Don't neglect this part of your health.

YIELDS A HIGH RETURN

© 1994 by The Standard Publishing Company. Permission is granted to reproduce this page for ministry purposes only—not for resale.

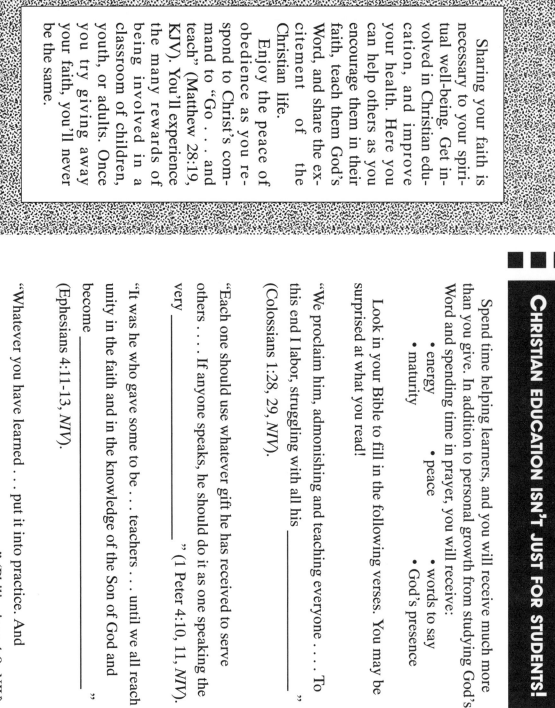

Sharing your faith is necessary to your spiritual well-being. Get involved in Christian education, and improve your health. Here you can help others as you encourage them in their faith, teach them God's Word, and share the excitement of the Christian life.

Enjoy the peace of obedience as you respond to Christ's command to "Go . . . and teach" (Matthew 28:19, KJV). You'll experience the many rewards of being involved in a classroom of children, youth, or adults. Once you try giving away your faith, you'll never be the same.

CHRISTIAN EDUCATION ISN'T JUST FOR STUDENTS!

Spend time helping learners, and you will receive much more than you give. In addition to personal growth from studying God's Word and spending time in prayer, you will receive:

- energy
- maturity
- peace
- words to say
- God's presence

Look in your Bible to fill in the following verses. You may be surprised at what you read!

"We proclaim him, admonishing and teaching everyone . . . . To this end I labor, struggling with all his _____" (Colossians 1:28, 29, NIV).

"Each one should use whatever gift he has received to serve others . . . . If anyone speaks, he should do it as one speaking the very _____" (1 Peter 4:10, 11, NIV).

"It was he who gave some to be . . . teachers . . . until we all reach unity in the faith and in the knowledge of the Son of God and become _____" (Ephesians 4:11-13, NIV).

"Whatever you have learned . . . put it into practice. And _____" (Philippians 4:9, NIV).

"Go ye therefore, and teach all nations . . . and, lo, I am _____" (Matthew 28:19, 20, KJV).

I'd like to have some of these benefits. Please give me some more information.

Name   Telephone

From Survey to Recruiting Success

What, another survey? Before you use a survey (an excellent, non-threatening recruiting tool) look at some of these frequently heard comments.

Why should I fill this out? The church already has my address.
Clearly explain the purpose and future use of the information asked for. A survey for potential teachers asks for *information only*, not for commitment to an unknown task. For example: "If you are interested in learning what's involved in one or more of the following ministries, please check below. Someone who knows that ministry will contact you to explain it and answer any questions you may have. Your check here is not a commitment, but a request for information."

I can't teach, and I can't sing. I don't want to work with children. What else is there for me to do?
Instead of providing a different survey for each department (music, education, missions) include ministry opportunities from all areas of the church in one presentation. Not only does this remind us of the variety of ministry possibilities, it illustrates that each different ministry gift contributes to one body of believers. God has designed His church with a ministry for each believer.

Include ministries that are not as public as teaching or singing. Consider how individuals can be included such as prayer partners for the kindergarten class, class parent to assist in special events, telephoners, or readers for senior adults. The recruiter's ministry is to help everyone take part, not just to provide teachers for established classes.

I filled out one of these things last time. Why do I have to do another?
Use *new* questions and give the survey form a *new* appearance to eliminate this reaction. We all resist repetition, and if something looks familiar we may not read far enough to see that it is different. Design a new survey each time by using a different size and color of paper and a different format. Put the name and address at the bottom this year, or use a new typeface and style of illustrations.

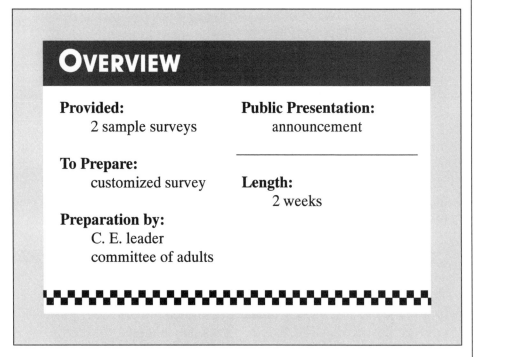

OVERVIEW

Provided:
2 sample surveys

To Prepare:
customized survey

Preparation by:
C. E. leader
committee of adults

Public Presentation:
announcement

Length:
2 weeks

Planning

Two sample surveys are provided here, but it is best to customize your own survey to meet your specific program needs. As you design the survey, remember that many people react negatively to surveys. Word it carefully. Survey your congregation once a year, preferably during a Sunday morning service.

Announcement

When you introduce the survey to the congregation, explain how it will be used. Provide an opportunity for questions to be asked and ways for privacy to be respected. If possible, have the survey completed immediately and collected during the same service.

Follow-up

After you have designed, presented, and collected the surveys, the talking begins. Ask several people to help you. Find those who are concerned that every believer have a place to serve and who are also well acquainted with the possibilities for ministry within your congregation. Meet for prayer and discussion of what to say when contacting those surveyed.

Organize the completed survey forms so that *everyone* receives a telephone call or other personal contact. The success of your survey depends on what you do *after* you receive the information. Talk about ministry opportunities, training that will be provided, and team support for those who are committed to Christian service.

The personal interest shown after a survey makes this an effective recruiting tool. With God's direction and guidance you will have the privilege of sharing His work with many new people.

INTEREST SURVEY

Name _____ Occupation _____

Address _____ City _____ Zip _____

Telephone Number (day) _____ (evening) _____

Age (Check one.)   Marital Status _____
___ young teen
___ high school   Is this church your primary place of worship? yes ____ no ____
___ 18-24
___ 25-29   If yes, how long have you attended? less than 6 months ___ over 6 months ___
___ 30's
___ 40's   Services you regularly attend _____
___ 50's
___ 60's   _____
___ 70+

You Are a Minister!
Mark the following with **P** for previous experience, **I** for interested, or **C** for currently involved.

CHILDREN'S MINISTRY   MUSIC MINISTRY
Preferred age group   ___ choir
___ nursery   ___ solos
___ early childhood (ages 2-5)   ___ instrumental
___ elementary (ages 6-12)   ___ sound system
Preferred time(s)   ___ drama
___ Sunday morning   ___ children
___ Sunday evening   ___ youth
___ weekdays
___ special events   HOSPITALITY
                                        ___ usher
YOUTH MINISTRY   ___ greeter
Preferred age   ___ telephoning
___ young teen   ___ visitation
___ high school   ___ prayer chain
___ college   ___ letter-writing

ADULT MINISTRY   I CAN OFFER THESE SKILLS:
___ Sunday school   ___ gardening
___ small groups   ___ cooking
___ women's interests   ___ driving
___ men's interests   ___ typing/computer
___ singles   ___ other _____
___ seniors

Comments _____

_____

© 1994 by The Standard Publishing Company. Permission is granted to reproduce this page for ministry purposes only—not for resale.

SURVEY

Name _____ Phone (day) _____ (eve) _____

Address _____ City _____ Zip _____

Please complete these sentences.
We are very interested in what you are thinking!

1. If I could do anything I wanted to help this church be a better place, I would

    _____ .

2. I would like to recommend _____ (name)

    to serve as _____ (position).

3. As a parent, I think _____

    _____ .

There are opportunities available for you here.
Please tell us how you would like to be involved by checking choices below.

Please check:
    I would like information about
    ___ teaching, ___ assisting, or ___ being a substitute teacher.

The age level I am most interested in is:
___ nursery   ___ college age (18-24 years)
___ early childhood (ages 2-5)   ___ adult
___ elementary (ages 6-12)   ___ singles
___ young teen   ___ seniors
___ high school

Please tell me how I can minister using these skills:
___ driving   ___ sewing
___ cooking   ___ housecleaning
___ typing/computer   ___ financial planning
___ plumbing   ___ telephoning
___ maintenance/buildings and grounds
___ other _____

_____

© 1994 by The Standard Publishing Company. Permission is granted to reproduce this page for ministry purposes only—not for resale.

THE "GENERATION CHAIN"

Granny Mathews taught Sunday school and touched lives for God for 90 years before she died recently at age 101. She taught Phil in children's church and gave him his first Bible. As a minister of Christian education, Phil now teaches teachers. Among them is Pat, who shares Jesus with a group of children each week in children's church.

Granny Mathews, Phil, and Pat are examples of God's plan for teaching, as described in Psalm 78:

> We will tell the next generation the praiseworthy deeds of the Lord, his power, and the wonders he has done . . . . He commanded our forefathers to teach their children, so the next generation would know them, even the children yet to be born, and they in turn would tell their children. Then they would put their trust in God and would not forget his deeds but would keep his commands (Psalm 78:4-7).

Psalm 78 is illustrated in our Sunday schools every week. Use this concept to help recruit new teachers. Recognizing ourselves as a part of the "Generation Chain" described in Psalm 78 helps us to see and understand the significance of the teaching ministry.

This recruiting plan includes quotes about the influence of specific teachers, interviews with at least one "Generation Chain," and a call for others in the congregation to link up.

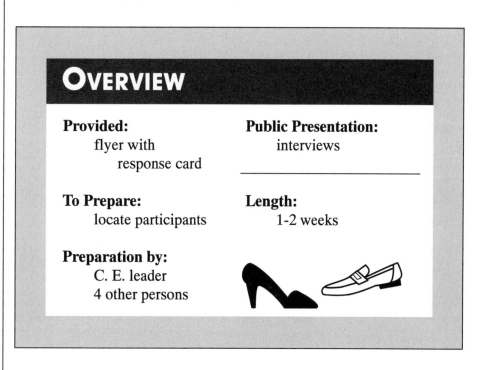

OVERVIEW

Provided:
flyer with
response card

To Prepare:
locate participants

Preparation by:
C. E. leader
4 other persons

Public Presentation:
interviews

Length:
1-2 weeks

Planning

Start by locating those in your church who are part of a Psalm 78 "Generation Chain." As you are talking with people about their experiences, ask specific questions about the teachers they remember. Why were these teachers memorable?

Here are several ways to find these individuals:

Senior adults—Talk to older adults about their teaching experiences. Ask about the teachers they had during their younger years.

Current teaching staff—Ask them for names of teachers who influenced them in Sunday school.

General announcement—Place a notice in church publications, or make a verbal announcement that you need information about Sunday school teachers who influenced the lives of people in your church.

Optional Presentations

Ask people for statements about the teachers they remember. As you gather these stories, put a few in the church bulletin or mailer under the heading, "Teachers Who Live On." Use one or two a week for several weeks before the public interviews.

Presentation Sunday

Choose a Sunday to interview a "Generation Chain" of teaching. Have at least four generations (related or unrelated) talk about how God has used teachers to help them as Christians. Use a senior adult, a middle-aged adult, a young adult, and a child.

Have someone—perhaps the child in the chain—read Psalm 78:1-8. Then explain that this psalm comes to life in your church every week. The visual impact is powerful—one generation telling the next generation, telling the next, telling the next, and so on.

Briefly interview each of the "links" in this chain, asking why they would recommend Sunday school teaching to those not yet involved.

Psalm 78 is God's design. Make it a visual recruiting tool. As you and your generation chain show how God uses people to minister, you can help others become part of this design.

Then ask the congregation to consider prayerfully whether God is asking them to be a part of a Psalm 78 chain. One can join at any age and become a part of telling the next generation, even if one begins later in life.

Flyer

Copy the flyer from page 67 after adding your church name, address, and telephone number. Be sure to include instructions verbally or in writing for returning the response card. For example:

> **Tear off the bottom portion after you have filled it in and give it to the host at the information booth in the church lobby.**
>
> Call _____(person)_____ at _____(telephone number)_____ for more information.

Distribute the flyer and response card. Since most people need additional information before making a decision, explain that an expression of interest is not a commitment but only a request for more details.

Follow-up

As soon as possible, contact all those who have expressed an interest on the response card. Discuss the opportunities for ministry, time for prayer before decisions are made, and the training and observation time provided. Direct each interested person to others who can answer questions and give appropriate guidance about a commitment to ministry.

GOD'S "GENERATION CHAIN"

Psalm 78:1-7 *(NIV)*

O my people, hear my teaching;
  listen to the words of my mouth.

I will open my mouth in parables,
  I will utter hidden things, things from of old—

what we have heard and known,
  what our fathers have told us.

We will not hide them from their children;
  we will tell the next generation
the praiseworthy deeds of the Lord,
  his power, and the wonders he has done.

He decreed statutes for Jacob
  and established the law in Israel,
which he commanded our forefathers
  to teach their children,

so the next generation would know them,
  even the children yet to be born,
  and they in turn would tell their children.

Then they would put their trust in God
  and would not forget his deeds
  but would keep his commands.

I'm a part of God's "Generation Chain."

How can I be a link in our church's Bible education? Please call me about more information.

_____

Name   Telephone Number

© 1994 by The Standard Publishing Company. Permission is granted to reproduce this page for ministry purposes only—not for resale.

"Will you teach the Primaries for a quarter?"

"We need a youth coordinator. Will you volunteer?"

"Join our teaching team. Our quarterly gives you lots of help to make teaching easy."

As the recruiter of new Sunday school teachers, are you aware of your words? Do you use an "educationese" vocabulary the public does not understand?

Your first goal is to expand your teaching staff. You want to give additional people the joy and privilege of ministry through teaching. This means you will be recruiting from three different groups of adults: (1) new Christians, (2) those who have moved to your church from another area, and (3) members of your congregation who are strong in their faith but not active in ministry.

Even the latter group may not be familiar with terms we use. They can easily be confused by our announcements. Instead of avoiding or changing our everyday education jargon, use it as an attention-getting recruiting tool.

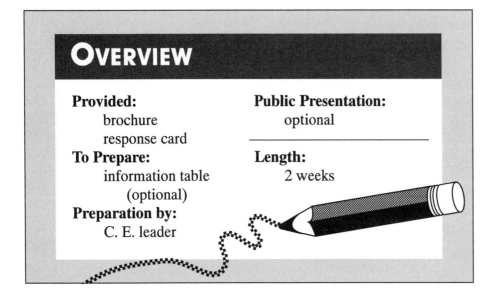

OVERVIEW

Provided:
   brochure
   response card

To Prepare:
   information table
      (optional)

Preparation by:
   C. E. leader

Public Presentation:
   optional

Length:
   2 weeks

Add your church name, address, and telephone number to the back of the brochure on pages 69 and 70. You may need to add or change the quiz questions to fit your congregation and your local terminology. Then copy the two-sided brochure and fold it in half. Use this as a special handout with a response card (see page 71) enclosed. Add directions for returning the card to the bottom of each card.

Distribute this brochure on two consecutive Sundays or mail it to the church's mailing list.

For effective recruiting, it is *essential* that you respond to all calls and cards you receive. Most people will reach out tentatively to inquiry about becoming involved. Then it is up to you as the recruiter to take the next step and help them move toward ministry.

Brochure and Response Card

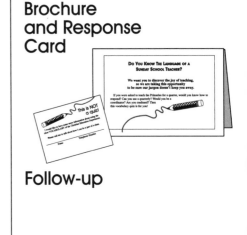

Follow-up

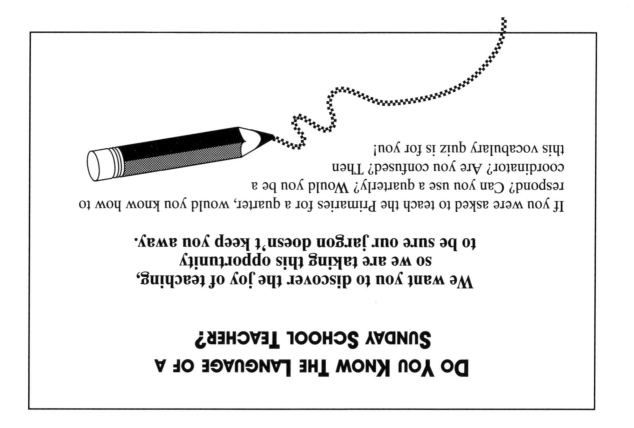

Do You Know The Language of A Sunday School Teacher?

We want you to discover the joy of teaching, so we are taking this opportunity to be sure our jargon doesn't keep you away.

If you were asked to teach the Primaries for a quarter, would you know how to respond? Can you use a quarterly? Would you be a coordinator? Are you confused? Then this vocabulary quiz is for you!

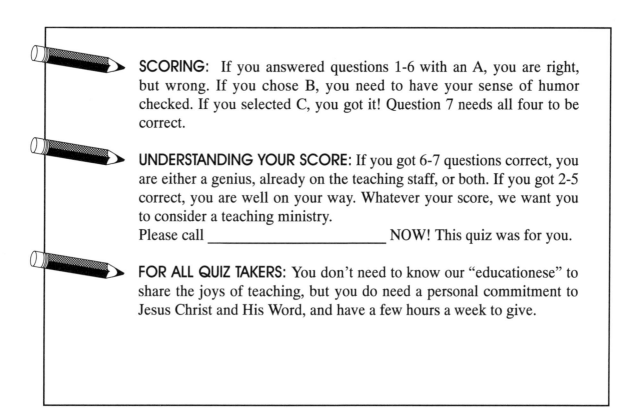

SCORING: If you answered questions 1-6 with an A, you are right, but wrong. If you chose B, you need to have your sense of humor checked. If you selected C, you got it! Question 7 needs all four to be correct.

UNDERSTANDING YOUR SCORE: If you got 6-7 questions correct, you are either a genius, already on the teaching staff, or both. If you got 2-5 correct, you are well on your way. Whatever your score, we want you to consider a teaching ministry.
Please call _____ NOW! This quiz was for you.

FOR ALL QUIZ TAKERS: You don't need to know our "educationese" to share the joys of teaching, but you do need a personal commitment to Jesus Christ and His Word, and have a few hours a week to give.

© 1994 by The Standard Publishing Company. Permission is granted to reproduce this page for ministry purposes only—not for resale.

Mark the response you think best defines the meaning of each word.

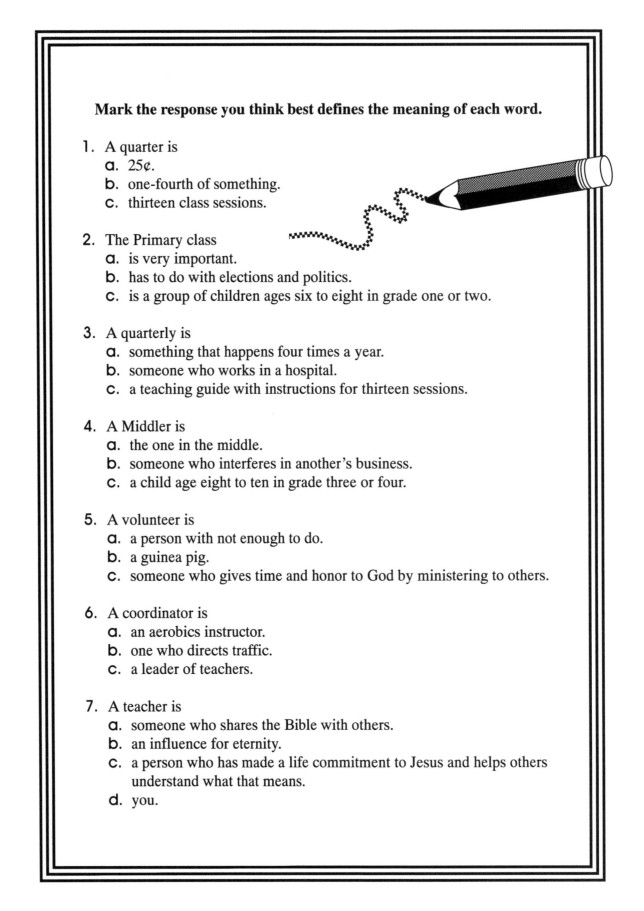

1. A quarter is
    a. 25¢.
    b. one-fourth of something.
    c. thirteen class sessions.

2. The Primary class
    a. is very important.
    b. has to do with elections and politics.
    c. is a group of children ages six to eight in grade one or two.

3. A quarterly is
    a. something that happens four times a year.
    b. someone who works in a hospital.
    c. a teaching guide with instructions for thirteen sessions.

4. A Middler is
    a. the one in the middle.
    b. someone who interferes in another's business.
    c. a child age eight to ten in grade three or four.

5. A volunteer is
    a. a person with not enough to do.
    b. a guinea pig.
    c. someone who gives time and honor to God by ministering to others.

6. A coordinator is
    a. an aerobics instructor.
    b. one who directs traffic.
    c. a leader of teachers.

7. A teacher is
    a. someone who shares the Bible with others.
    b. an influence for eternity.
    c. a person who has made a life commitment to Jesus and helps others understand what that means.
    d. you.

© 1994 by The Standard Publishing Company. Permission is granted to reproduce this page for ministry purposes only—not for resale.

Response Card

This is NOT a quiz!

I would like to have some more information about using the clear VOCABULARY of the Christian Education Department.

Please call me to talk about how I can be a part of a class.

_____
Name

_____
Telephone Number

This is NOT a quiz!

I would like to have some more information about using the clear VOCABULARY of the Christian Education Department.

Please call me to talk about how I can be a part of a class.

_____
Name

_____
Telephone Number

This is NOT a quiz!

I would like to have some more information about using the clear VOCABULARY of the Christian Education Department.

Please call me to talk about how I can be a part of a class.

_____
Name

_____
Telephone Number

This is NOT a quiz!

I would like to have some more information about using the clear VOCABULARY of the Christian Education Department.

Please call me to talk about how I can be a part of a class.

_____
Name

_____
Telephone Number

© 1994 by The Standard Publishing Company. Permission is granted to reproduce this page for ministry purposes only—not for resale.

Section 3
Read This When . . .

Recruiting is an ongoing ministry. You, as a recruiter, frequently face new challenges, often experience some discouragement, and look for new ways of approaching another season of finding new teachers.

Since your challenges are so varied, you may need a new look at what to do next. If you are looking for one new teacher to fill an immediate opening, you will not recruit the same way as if you need thirty new teachers who will begin in three months.

Select readings now to meet your immediate needs. Then keep Section 3 at your fingertips for when you need it later.

READ THIS WHEN . . .

READ THIS WHEN . . .
You Hear Only "No" to Your Requests

Listen to the "No's"

"**I**'M VERY HAPPY SERVING AS THE recruiter for new teachers and leaders in our Sunday school. It's just that I haven't been able to persuade anyone to say *yes*. Everyone I talk to is either too busy or doesn't seem to know how important all this is. I'm really not sure how to respond to these people. Do you have some suggestions for me? How can I make a *yes* out of a *no*?"

It's difficult when you receive a negative response, isn't it? However, we need to remember that we aren't asking people to get involved in Sunday school to help us, but as service to God. Each person is responsible to God for his or her *yes* or *no* and that makes your task a lot easier. But let's talk about why people are saying *no* instead of *yes*.

At some point every Christian education administrator faces the challenge to motivate people for service to God. Although the final response is between the individual and the Lord, we have the responsibility of presenting the need for service.

Here are some of the reasons for someone saying, "No, I don't want to become involved."

"I don't think it's for me. I need to learn more first."

Many people don't know the importance of service in their relationship to God. Christian growth takes place when we give of ourselves and what we have learned from the Lord.

A significant part of recruiting is letting Christians, especially new ones, know *why* they should be serving. Lay the groundwork first. As the Holy Spirit speaks to each person about ministry, recruitment will be greater. We need to teach the ministry side of our salvation, that service to Christ is not an option. Congregations are composed of people from a variety of backgrounds. Because everyone is at a different level of spiritual maturity, we cannot assume that each one knows what the

Scriptures teach about service to God.

"I'm too busy."

We are all tempted to use this excuse. Listen carefully to those who explain why they can't serve. Perhaps the demands on their lives are such that additional responsibility is not appropriate. Usually, however, prayer and a gentle reminder help people evaluate priorities.

"I'm involved in other areas of ministry."

Some people may not respond to your request for help because they are involved in ministry in other areas. Teaching a Bible study at work or visiting a retirement center regularly are also vital ministries to the church. Express your appreciation to those who are already in service, and recognize that a *no* to you can still be a *yes* to the Lord.

"I don't know how."

This response leads you to talk directly about your training programs and opportunities to observe and work with experienced teachers. Building the confidence of a new teacher or helper is a way to show your support.

Successful recruiting means finding the right person to do the right thing at the right time. You can make a *yes* out of a *no* by listening carefully. Teach about our ongoing relationship with God, meet the needs expressed in people's responses, and get ready to train new teachers.

And now, O Israel, what does the Lord your God ask of you but to fear the Lord your God, to walk in all his ways, to love him, to serve the Lord your God with all your heart and with all your soul, and to observe the Lord's commands and decrees that I am giving you today for your own good? (Deuteronomy 10:12, 13).

Therefore go and make disciples of all nations, baptizing them in the name of the Father and of the Son and of the Holy Spirit, and teaching them to obey everything I have commanded you. And surely I am with you always, to the very end of the age (Matthew 28:19, 20).

These two verses illustrate that the Word of God is clear about our responsibility to be an active part of Christ's church. (See also 1 Samuel 12:24; Ephesians 6:7, 8; James 1:22; 1 Peter 4:10, 11.)

You Suspect You Need to Change Your Ministry

"Do you think recruiting has a bad name?" the leader asked a group of Sunday school superintendents and Christian education ministers attending an interdenominational Sunday school conference recently. Their response was an emphatic *yes!*

Then they were asked to explain why recruiting has a negative image.

"Think about how you were recruited," one remarked. "I was recruited with no specific information as to what was involved or how long I would be doing it. If everyone is recruited the same way I was, no wonder recruiting is a bad word."

Another spoke, "People in our church avoid me because they think I will ask them to teach or something. As a recruiter, I don't feel welcome in any group." This comment drew agreement from many.

"I have to admit it," said another. "I'm always looking for teachers. We have a real need because our church is growing. That's good, but because I take any help I can get, I'm probably perpetuating the bad name."

Can this bad reputation of recruiters and recruiting be changed? It's possible, but it will take some work. As leaders we need to examine our own attitudes about recruiting, because we hold the potential for making recruiting exciting.

If recruiting is your least favorite part of being a Sunday school administrator, check your definition.

Does recruiting mean: (a) finding people to do what needs to be done, or (b) helping people find their places of ministry in the church?

The bad reputation recruiting has won't change until we focus on ministry and people, instead of on merely filling positions. Here are some suggestions that will help.

Are You Giving Recruiting a Bad Name?

Spread Enthusiasm About Ministry

"Serve the Lord with gladness" (Psalm 100:2, *KJV*). Discover what the Lord is doing now through people in your church. Ask everyone currently involved in ministry to share with others the exciting and positive things that are happening each week.

Remind the staff how damaging negative stories and criticism are, and discuss the value of spreading excitement throughout the church body. Talk about the significance of being a part of God's work. This excitement is inspiring to those not involved. You will help your reputation as a recruiter if you focus on excitement.

Form a Group of Recruiters to Work With You

Locate personable, warm adults who are comfortable meeting new people. Share your methods, attitudes, and the best ways to begin initial recruiting conversations. Explain where to place the focus. For example, "This is an opportunity to explore areas of ministry. It is not a lifelong commitment."

Share your task of recruiting, and you'll also share its burdens and joys as you involve more people in ministry.

Show Respect for Volunteers

Can you honestly say that each person in your church is as important to God's kingdom as every other? As leaders we need to demonstrate God's unconditional love toward others. Accept people's family obligations, time restraints, and other limitations with understanding and support. Be flexible with scheduling to include those who have other commitments. The individuals you are recruiting will respond when they are aware of your respect for them and their contribution to the work of God.

Recruiting doesn't have to have a bad name. We are all involved in God's work. He is the source of our wisdom and creativity. As we ask Him for guidance, we will be effective in our ministry for the Lord.

READ THIS WHEN . . .

You Want Some Help

Do you have questions about recruiting new teachers? Does your church need a different approach from what it has used in the past?

Ask for recruiting ideas and suggestions from people outside the Sunday school or Christian Education Department. Many adults involved in other ministries have ideas and opinions to share, and some of them have been in your church long enough to know its history. Talking to them may give you a different angle on recruiting teachers and assistants to the Sunday school ministry.

Begin by creating a short-term task group of eight to ten individuals from the different adult groups in your church. Look for members whose diversity represents your congregation. Include at least one person from women's ministries, men's ministries, choir, adult Sunday school classes, mission groups, senior adults, and singles.

When you invite each person to be part of this group, explain that you will meet three times during the next two months. You are looking for ideas, evaluative thoughts, and constructive criticism about recruiting additional teachers and assistants for the Sunday school, but you are *not* recruiting them personally. Those on the task force are simply there to give the Christian Education Department a different perspective and to share from their experiences.

Before the first task group meeting, prepare a list of questions and distribute it among members of the group.

1. Why do we have Sunday school and Sunday school teachers?
2. How can we effectively communicate our need for additional teachers?
3. Do you think people know they can make a difference by teaching? If not, how can we communicate this?

Form a Task Group

When this group meets, spend a few minutes letting the members become better acquainted. Read 1 Corinthians 12:12-27 and discuss how this task group fits God's plan for ministry within His church. Although we are all part of the same church, we are gifted in different things. Not everyone is to be an "eye" or an "ear," but each can help the other parts of the body.

Show an interest in the personal ideas and opinions of group members. Talk through the questions on the list, using a brainstorming technique. Record suggestions on a chalkboard or overhead transparency without any negative comments or any evaluation. Ask additional questions to clarify meanings or to encourage additional discussion. First, "Do you think the congregation as a whole knows why we have Sunday school, and therefore, why we have teachers?" Depending on the group's response, brainstorm ways to begin or to continue emphasizing the value of the study of God's Word at all age levels. Besides collecting ideas and comments on a board, you may want to record the discussion on tape for later use.

Continue this brainstorming procedure with all questions, allowing time to explore new options before going on to the next item.

Before concluding the first meeting, set the date and place of a second meeting. The advantage of having at least two meetings is that thoughts and ideas arise after the first meeting. For many, the best ideas surface after they have had some time to process a group's interaction.

A few days after the first meeting mail a thank-you note to each person who participated. Summarize a few of the ideas discussed. Include the following questions to be considered and a reminder of the date and place of the next meeting.

1. How were you recruited to become a part of the group you are in? Why was it effective?
2. What recruiting methods excite you, motivate you, discourage you?
3. Who in your organization or group is not currently involved in leadership or other ministries, but might be interested in hearing about teaching or other opportunities in the Sunday school?

Let the group's ideas and suggestions establish the pattern for each meeting. Decide if additional meetings would be helpful. Remind each participant of the valuable contribution he is making to the ministry.

A task group that can provide new ideas will be a blessing to you as the recruiter of teachers. You will feel the love and prayer support of others within God's church and experience 1 Corinthians 12 in action.

READ THIS WHEN . . .

Christian Education
Seems to Be a Hidden Ministry

S-E-E-ing Helps Recruiting

Are all the people in your congregation able to *see* Sunday school? Are Sunday school teaching and other activities evident throughout your facilities?

"It isn't easy to *see* Sunday school in our church. All the teaching takes place in the classrooms, either in the education wing or downstairs. How can you *see* the Sunday school when most of it takes place behind closed doors?"

"I wonder if our church has a class for young adults. I've only heard about the classes for children, but now that my own kids are older, I'd enjoy helping with young adults."

When everyone—of all ages and interests—can *see* what is going on in the church, your recruiting efforts will be rewarded with more new teachers and assistants. Think about what you can do to make the Sunday school more visible. Is it possible for everyone in your congregation to *see* it in action—a lively, exciting place, with learners growing spiritually in knowledge and experience?

Start by looking at your church as if you were a newcomer wanting to learn about the educational opportunities. What would you like to *see*? Set some *see* goals. For example, decide to do something every other month to make the Sunday school visible to the church body throughout the church facilities.

Here are some ways to help others *see* the Sunday school.

Show classes, teachers, and learners in action. Take the Sunday school classes outside the classroom and show them off. If you want to help everyone *see* what goes on inside the room, use videos, slides, and photographs. Photograph some of the classes and creatively share the material. Post photographs on bulletin boards or enlarge them to poster size. Display slides with a repeat projector on a table in the lobby. Show a video in small groups or at meetings throughout the week.

You can also show action by taking the students outside of the classroom. Plan for children to visit the adults or vice versa. Organize skits, art displays, memory presentations, music sharing, and other methods appropriate for your classes and facilities. Generate new ideas for taking classes outside their walls.

Encourage current participants to talk about their experiences. We all like to be a part of something exciting and rewarding. Design some ways for the teachers and assistants to talk about what God is doing in their classes. Provide interview opportunities at various times with various formats such as minister to teacher, teacher to teacher, parent to teacher, learner to teacher, and so forth. Have a third person tell someone else's story to give a different perspective.

Schedule an open house of classrooms to let everyone tell what goes on each week. Students and teachers can share the excitement of learning as they talk about what they do.

Enlarge the vision for the life-changing effects of studying God's Word. Print the testimonies of some of your senior adults. Have them tell how God has helped them grow through His Word. Use one or two stories at a time in different publications. Mail these or distribute them at the church. Use flyers, postcards, letters, and the church bulletin to share the effects of being involved in Sunday school, either as a student or a teacher. Let people know that God is at work in His church.

As you use *see* Sunday school ideas, try for as much variety as possible. Ask God to help you bring glory to Him by showing you new ways to demonstrate what He is doing in the lives of those in Sunday school. Be sure that all age groups are represented.

Seeing your Sunday school in action will encourage people to participate. When they know more about this exciting opportunity to share God's Word with others, your recruiting efforts will be rewarded with new teachers and leaders.

You Wonder If Recruiting Is Ever Fun

"I really enjoy being a recruiter," says Kate O'Donnell, a Minister of Christian Education in Ocean Beach, California. "Making the perfect fit between the person and the ministry need is always a *joy*."

"In my congregation, we have a young man helping in children's ministries. You should see him with the children; it is obvious that God has gifted him for this," Kate exclaims. "There is such *joy* in his face! You can tell that he's having a grand time and God's love is speaking to those children.

The Joys of Recruiting

It was wonderful knowing that God was guiding us when I discussed our Christian education needs with him, and he said he'd try working with children."

Kate describes recruiting as "finding the perfect mesh between somebody's spiritual gifts and the needs in our church." She says her job is to learn how to blend these two elements. As part of her recruiting plan she is careful to give new prospects plenty of time to pray and consider how God is asking them to serve. Kate knows it is more important to discover each person's attitude toward the church and personal spiritual growth than just to find someone to fill a role in a classroom.

"As the Minister of Christian Education, my responsibility goes beyond recruiting. Once someone is recruited and trained to fill a ministry role, my job isn't over. I feel responsible for helping him or her continue to grow as a disciple, experiencing Christ's *joy* personally—not just improving the staff of the Christian Education Department."

Focus your recruiting on the *joys* of service as you follow Kate's example of ministering to her current and future staff.

"The Feature Teacher" is one way Kate O'Donnell spreads the *joy* of ministry. This monthly presentation honors a teacher and continues to inform the congregation about the blessings of service to God. Each month Kate gives an honored teacher a coffee mug that bears the slogan, "I love teaching God's Word." Then the teacher shares some personal teaching experiences.

"The testimony is always the best part." Kate says. "It is encouraging to everyone to hear how God is working during class time and in the lives of students. The message always comes across that the teacher is receiving as much or more than he or she is giving."

"What these 'Featured Teachers' say about the *joy* they find in teaching is *my* reward each month," Kate continues. "Recruiting them for service was just the beginning."

Be encouraged as you consider the *joys* of recruiting. As you continue to help believers find their place of ministry, you are ministering to them. Your *joy* in the Lord will be contagious.

These Bible verses can help you make your congregation aware of the supernatural *joy* of service. Create a bulletin board display featuring one of the verses with pictures from some classes in action. Use the theme of *joy* in your newsletters and Sunday bulletin inserts when you discuss the need for additional teachers. *Joy* is contagious. Share with the congregation some of the *joyous* experiences of your staff.

"Worship the Lord with gladness; come before him with joyful songs" (Psalm 100:2).

"For the kingdom of God is not a matter of eating and drinking, but of righteousness, peace and joy in the Holy Spirit, because anyone who serves Christ in this way is pleasing to God and approved by men" (Romans 14:17, 18).

"If you obey my commands, you will remain in my love, just as I have obeyed my Father's commands and remain in his love. I have told you this so that my joy may be in you and that your joy may be complete" (John 15:10, 11).

READ THIS WHEN . . .

You Can't Find the "Perfect" Teacher

Hold Your Tongue
Words to AVOID When You Are Recruiting

You have just completed a successful recruiting program, and several potential teachers have responded. You are now planning training sessions and opportunities for these recruits to observe in the classrooms. You are excited that they are interested in becoming part of the Christian education program.

However, several of these new volunteers are not as talented as you would like, and you want to maintain the high standard of quality that teaching deserves. What do you do when your appeal for teachers attracts those who do not fit your image of the "ideal teacher"? What do you say to them?

Anything goes when you are recruiting, so you have to tell it like it is. Right? Wrong! When someone responds with a desire to become involved in ministry, you may have to watch your words carefully. Here are some things you should *not* say.

DON'T SAY, "YOU ARE NOT QUALIFIED."

Although not everyone is capable of teaching a group of people, everyone *is* qualified to be involved in some area of ministry. As a recruiter, you have the responsibility before God to help each person work toward an appropriate use of his or her abilities and talents. Romans 12:5, 6 teaches, "So in Christ we who are many form one body, and each member belongs to all the others. We have different gifts, according to the grace given us." It would be terrible to deny someone a place of service within the church body.

You can avoid saying, "You are not qualified," by the words you use in your publicity and recruiting efforts. Rather than saying, "If you are interested in being the fourth grade Sunday school teacher, please see me," make your announcements broad enough to include ministry opportunities other than lead teacher. Say, "Our children are looking forward to having several adults share the Sunday school hour with them. If God is speaking to you about being a part of this ministry, please see me."

It takes more effort and planning, but many of the Christian Education Department tasks can be delegated to those not gifted as teachers. Ask God for guidance and creativity, and make a list of options. You won't ever have to say, "You are not qualified."

DON'T SAY, "WE DON'T NEED ANY MORE PEOPLE RIGHT NOW."

If your classrooms are adequately staffed without using everyone who has volunteered, thank God! However, *never* turn away those who do not fit into a teaching position. There are many ways to use one more person. First, consider giving one of the long-term teachers a short leave of absence. Add another assistant to your largest group to have a better teacher-learner ratio. Use this additional volunteer as a permanent substitute, always on call for any class when needed.

Include everyone who is interested as often as you can. With an inevitable turnover in some are as of leadership, you should be training additional volunteers on an ongoing basis.

DON'T SAY, "YOU ARE TOO OLD."

Many older adults are outstanding teachers and a vital part of the education ministry. Other seniors are not actively involved and may even need to be reminded they are wanted and needed. No one is too old to be a part of the church, and no one is too old to serve.

Ask God to help you think of areas where an older person may be effective. Then you will have several options when you are tempted to say, "You are too old." A faithful assistant is needed in many classes, especially those for children. Add rocking chairs to the early childhood classrooms and ask seniors to provide hugs and laps as needed during a class time. Senior adults can go along on a class outing, make telephone calls, or help to prepare mailings. The needs are there, and everyone who is willing should have a place.

You have the responsibility for deciding the best places of ministry for the volunteer staff. God loves His church and is interested in who is teaching and influencing His children. He will give you the guidance you need. Be careful about your words. We are all sensitive about our abilities or lack of them.

Although a few things should be left unsaid, there are still many words that can be shared with your congregation. Helping someone take the initial step toward ministry involvement is rewarding as well as challenging. Share the excitement of serving God with your words, prayers of encouragement, and support. You'll be amazed at how God will lead new workers into His service.

Your Old System Isn't Working

Update Your Recruiting Methods

"This year I am having trouble finding teachers for Sunday school. Everyone is too busy. We've made announcements, but no one responds. We just can't find teachers. I don't know what to do!"

I received this response recently from leaders in several neighboring churches when I innocently asked, "How is it going?" The discouraged words of these recruiters are familiar. It does seem more difficult to find volunteers. Maybe the old ways aren't working anymore. I asked some questions about their recruiting methods.

"Have you recruited by talking to someone personally—such as parents or new members?"

"Well, no."

"Have you put something in the bulletin or printed a brochure that explains *why* people should teach?"

"Well, no."

"Have you prayed for guidance in choosing a recruiting approach?"

"Well, not really. I pray that people will come to me to ask about getting involved."

Maybe it is harder now to find new teachers in your congregation, but that must challenge you to be more creative and alert to recruiting techniques.

All recruiting must begin with prayer. God is vitally interested in the work of His church and His people. As our Creator, He provides ideas to help us minister. God has established the plan of using people to teach His church. Depend on God in times of difficult recruiting.

Because churches and congregations differ, some recruiting ideas may be effective in one community and not appropriate for another. Ask God to help you make teaching His Word a priority to those in your congregation. Do you have experienced, mature, older believers who don't volunteer because of their ages, but who would be delighted to help if they were personally asked? Do you have young families who need customized schedules and planning assistance? Is your Sunday school an exciting place of learning that appeals to various groups? God has the ideal plan for the group of people you worship with each week.

Since my youth, O God, you have taught me, and to this day I declare your marvelous deeds. Even when I am old and gray, do not forsake me, O God, till I declare your power to the next generation, your might to all who are to come (Psalm 71:17, 18).

David presents one reason for being involved in teaching others. We have been taught the wonderful truth of who God is, and experienced the blessing of that relationship; it is our responsibility then to teach others. How better can we express our gratitude to Him than to share salvation?

Use Psalm 71 and other Bible passages to communicate *why* we teach. Help people understand that teaching others isn't something we do if we have extra time; it is to be a priority in our own Christian growth.

Besides prayer and God's Word, include a personal touch to influence potential teachers. A face-to-face invitation is the most effective way to involve new people in your education department. Ask God to lead you to those He wants as teachers, and become acquainted with them.

Many parents want to give time because they are interested in the spiritual education of their families. They may be reluctant to add something else to their busy schedules. Still, if you explain the need and are open to flexible scheduling, you will find some new teachers. National statistics about volunteers in churches and secular organizations show that most work full time, have busy family lives, and are between the ages of 25 and 45.

Don't be shy about talking to parents. They already have an interest in what is happening in the classrooms.

If you are concerned about where to find new Sunday school teachers, update your techniques. Ask God for custom methods, just for your congregation, and thank Him for being interested in the recruiting process. He is the source of both your encouragement and your ideas.

But as for me, I will always have hope; I will praise you more and more. My mouth will tell of your righteousness, of your salvation all day long, though I know not its measure. I will come and proclaim your mighty acts, O Sovereign Lord; I will proclaim your righteousness, yours alone (Psalm 71:14-16).

READ THIS WHEN . . .

You're the Only One Not on Vacation

Recruiting for Holidays and Vacations

"What do you do about Sunday school teachers on holiday weekends and vacations? I find it hard to recruit for those special occasions."

"I've just about given up on the in-between Sundays—like Christmas and August. Either the regular teachers are going out of town, or they can't teach for another reason."

A group of Sunday school leaders met for a brainstorming meeting to discover new ideas. Their discussion eventually focused on how to recruit for special weekends and what had to happen if recruiting would be effective.

When teachers are on a holiday or vacation, frequently the students are too. Attendance may be higher or lower, and there is usually a change in attention span, especially with children. The "holiday spirit" may affect what is planned for classes.

Holidays and vacation seasons often include changes in the scheduling and grouping of classes. These details need to be considered and planned for *before* recruiting for holidays and vacations can begin.

"We have a summer program that is more like a club than regular Sunday school. The children rotate from room to room—hear a story in one room, have singing and worship in another, and so on. It's a great change for everyone."

The conclusion of the leader's discussion was that recruiting should move to *fourth* place in the action steps. Here's what to do.

▲ First, look at the history.
▲ Second, pray for guidance.
▲ Third, plan for changes.
▲ Fourth, recruit if necessary.

▲ **Look at Your Sunday School History**

What do your records from the past few years for the same time period tell you? Compared with the rest of the year, did the attendance change? In what way? How many regular teachers asked for substitutes? What special events, such as choir rehearsals or children's programs, affected the class length or curricula? What things have you done in the past that were effective? What should you not repeat? Make notes from your Sunday school's recent history. Look for a pattern to help you plan for this year.

▲ Pray

As you consider what you have learned from looking at the recent history of your Sunday school, ask God for guidance. Pray for the Holy Spirit to lead you to the people He is preparing as teachers for these special situations. Also pray for guidance about scheduling and what adjustments to make that will help the kingdom of God. Avoid those that won't be helpful to the students.

▲ Plan Ahead

Don't wait until the summer or a holiday is imminent to make changes in your grouping or schedule. Decide how many teachers and assistants you need to make the adjusted plan effective. You may undergo a complete change for a short period and need fewer teachers, or you may need a completely different staff. "We have combined several children's classes for the month of December and spent some time each week working on gifts for the children to distribute to needy families."

"Our adult classes have special guest speakers and occasionally a carefully selected video on holiday weekends."

"We have a summer program that is more like a club than regular Sunday school. The children rotate from room to room—hear a story in one room, have singing and worship in another, and so on. It's a great change for everyone."

As you plan for holidays and vacations, your recruiting needs will begin to take form. This leads you to the fourth stage.

▲ Recruit

You can now be much more specific when you make announcements, write publicity notices in your bulletin and mailer, or talk to new prospects about serving on your short-term or specialized staff. You know how many teachers you will need and what talents or experiences are needed.

Look for those you have contacted in the past who were unable to commit to a long-term teaching assignment. Contact parents, teenagers, college students home for brief periods, and senior adults. Professional teachers who may not be able to teach during the school year might enjoy short-term involvement. They are often interested in teaching a different skill and/or age group from their professional responsibilities.

People in your congregation want to be a part of planned, successful events and will contribute their time when it is clear what is needed. Use your Sunday school history and the guidance of the Holy Spirit to plan for the recruiting you need to do. Share the excitement of the holidays with everyone, and you'll be encouraged as new people become involved.

▲▲▲▲▲▲▲▲▲▲▲▲▲

You Think Recruiting Is All Bad News

The Good News and Bad News About the Volunteers You Recruit

Volunteerism is up! That's the good news.
In the past few years, the number of people volunteering time and energy has increased significantly. According to recent polls in *Newsweek* and the *Ladies' Home Journal*, nearly 50 percent of the people polled said that they volunteered some time each week for charity or an organization. That is up from 31 percent, less than ten years ago. Almost 90 million Americans donate at least three and a half hours each week to some voluntary, helping activity.

The polls state that the largest number of volunteers are adults ages 35-49. Also there are fewer women in these percentages than previous polls as more men are involved in volunteer projects.

Sunday school probably has the largest number of volunteers of any organization. It is good news for us, then, to learn that adults are more willing than ever to contribute time to worthwhile causes.

The bad news? Volunteers need some return for the time they give, and they need to know that what they give is worthwhile. The polls indicate that people are motivated to volunteer service if there is something received in exchange for their giving "above and beyond the expected." Although we in the church know of our eternal reward for our commitment to Christ, we also need to be aware of this natural, human need among volunteers.

What can we do to give some immediate return for the time volunteers offer to the church? There must be some indication from us and other leadership that each contribution is valuable. Send a personal note to teachers every few months, make a phone call to express appreciation, and encourage parents and class members to thank their leaders. This will give your volunteers a return for their time and help them see some immediate value for their contribution.

Provide frequent public recognition—some expression of appreciation. An annual banquet, a prayer of dedication in a public service, or printing a list of names in the bulletin are the most common methods of public commendation.

It is easier to recruit new volunteers when current teachers are excited about what they are doing. When morale is high in the Christian Education Department, the entire church benefits.

A volunteer is defined as one who works without payment, who may or may not be trained for the task, and who is motivated to give time. Do you fully appreciate those you are recruiting? Are you careful not to take their services for granted? Enjoy the good news about *more* people in volunteer service. Happy recruiting!

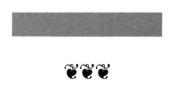

You Are Looking for an Easy Way Out

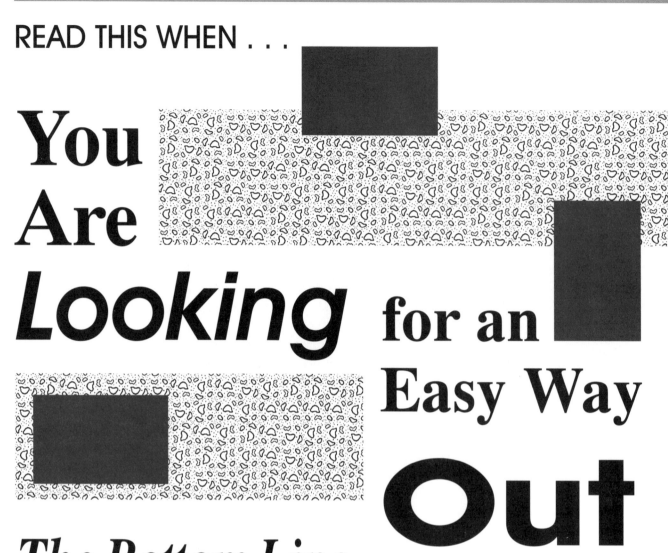

The Bottom Line

Recruiting was the subject of a recent round table discussion of Christian educators and leaders. Everyone talked about different methods to recruit new teachers. Some methods had been successful. Others helped spread the news of Christian education, but didn't recruit new teachers. Most participants agreed that they received very little response if they just made a public announcement about needing teachers. Recruiting must be preceded by publicity and public recognition.

Many new ideas were shared, and possibilities seemed unlimited. However, before the evening was over, everyone was asking the same questions: What really works? How can we consistently recruit new teachers? What is the "bottom line"?

To see if there is a "bottom line," we tried to learn from the personal experiences of the participants in the meeting. How had they become involved in teaching?

"How did you get started teaching Sunday school? Were you asked or did you tell someone you wanted to teach? Did you respond to an announcement about a need for teachers?"

The responses to these questions revealed much about human nature and gave us the help we needed in finding the "bottom line" of recruiting.

Fewer than ten percent of the attendees had responded to an announcement or request for teachers without a personal invitation. Over 90 percent said they taught their first Sunday school class because someone asked them to teach.

This surprising imbalance wasn't what we wanted to hear. As recruiters, we prefer to have new teachers come to us. It would be easier if we just made announcements, wrote brochures, sat back, and waited for responses. However, our informal survey at the leaders' round table illustrated that this method won't meet our need for teachers. The method that works, the "bottom line," is the individual, personal approach—asking people.

If successful recruiting means going to each individual, there are four other things that must be done *first*.

Pray

Before you approach anyone about involvement in teaching, ask God for guidance. This is the Lord's work, and He knows the needs of each class. Ask God to prepare hearts and give you wisdom. Pray for each individual as you recruit.

Ask the Potential Teacher to Pray for God's Leading

Suggest that the person spend a few days praying about the possibility of a teaching ministry. Do not make a specific request or expect an immediate commitment. God must speak to the one who will be teaching. Even if a temporary commitment is made, it amounts to a significant responsibility. This decision must include prayer and the proper concern.

Consider Personal Needs

As you begin the recruiting discussion, be sensitive to the commitments the person already has. Work and family responsibilities influence the amount of time a person can contribute. As you individualize your approach, be flexible and creative about the personal limitations and strengths. Place a high value on what each is able to contribute, rather than requiring everyone to fit one schedule or type of ministry. Your thoughtfulness will recruit more people to your teaching team.

Expect a "Yes"

After prayer by both you and the potential teacher and a sincere consideration of that person's responsibilities, you will usually receive a yes. Most people in your church want to be contributing members and will respond to the needs when they are presented. You will discover some who want to say yes but do not know how to contribute to the Lord's work. Your specific, individual request will be a welcome blessing. As you prayerfully talk to each person about the needs and opportunities in ministry, you can easily modify scheduling to fit the individual.

Check with your current teachers. Find out how many of them started to teach because someone asked. What are the percentages of those who were asked and those who offered? Is it similar to the group at the round table discussion? If so, then you know your "bottom line." Prayerfully ask God for guidance, and then go to the people. Your new teachers are waiting!

READ THIS WHEN . . .

> ## You Don't Think You'll Ever Find Teachers

Recruiting Requires Trust

Do you have enough *trust* to be an effective recruiter? If you are the one expected to find new teachers, where do you put your trust?

You may be thinking, "I know it will be impossible to get more teachers. I've already asked all the good prospects, and they are all too busy." Or, "Even though I've already talked to everyone I can think of, I'm going to continue to pray that God will speak to those He wants involved in Sunday school. I know God is concerned about His church."

Recruiting people to ministry opportunities is a challenging task. How you meet that challenge depends on your attitude of *trust*.

T—Trust God

"I'm so worried about all the new teachers we need. It is difficult to find anyone willing to make a commitment these days. I'm not sure what I'm going to do!"

Are you putting your trust in God to take care of the ministry needs of His church, or do you carry this responsibility by yourself? God loves the people in your congregation even more than you do, and He is concerned about the teaching ministry. Read Matthew 9:38 and Ephesians 4:11 to remind yourself that God sends the workers and gives the teachers to the church. When it seems no one is left to be recruited, thank God that the needs and challenges are His; you are just to follow His direction.

R—Respond First With Prayer

"Oh, no! We need two teachers by next week. Whom can I talk to first? Maybe Stuart will know someone. Where is his telephone number?"

As you put your trust in God to help you with the recruiting, remember that prayer is your first action. Matthew 9:38 tells us to "Ask the Lord . . . to send out workers." You show your trust as you continually bring your concerns, frustrations, and expectations to the Lord. He is the only one who can give you guidance for His church. As you begin your recruiting with prayer, you will also receive God's supernatural peace. This peace spreads to those you are enlisting, helping to give them confidence that this is a worthwhile ministry.

U—Understand That Each Person Is Responsible to God

"Yes, I know that you are involved in several other ministries, but we really need you to teach this year. You are such a good leader. Besides, I don't know who else to ask. Please say you'll do it; we're desperate."

Sometimes a response of no to your request for service is more appropriate than a yes. Your ministry is to do the praying, and then the asking, but it is up to each individual to answer the call from the Lord. Accept the decision of those involved in other ministries, knowing that various ministries are service unto God. If a person responds with no because of a lack of training or uncertainty about ability, explain the opportunities for help in these areas, and see if the no can become a yes.

S—Stress the Need for Prayer Before Commitment

"Sandra, would you consider getting involved with our young teens? I know you haven't had any experience, but I need someone to start this Sunday. Here are the materials. You'll do it, won't you?"

Even though your prayer for guidance is essential, it is not the only prayer needed. When you make that initial contact with a potential teacher, suggest that a few days be given to prayer about the decision before a commitment is made. Not only does this emphasize the importance of the commitment, but it puts the responsibility for the decision where it belongs— with the one who will do the teaching.

When you make general announcements and publish brochures to use as recruiting tools, focus on the need for prayer in God's plan for enlisting His people into His service. He knows the gifts and abilities He has given to His people, and He is concerned for the needs of those to be taught.

T—Trust God's People

"I know you think God is leading you to work with our youth, but this group needs someone with a lot of creativity. I think we should look for someone else."

As the people in your congregation are taught about their responsibility to be a part of the ministry of the church, expect God to answer their prayers for guidance. This may require that you be willing to help inexperienced or less capable persons become involved when they feel God is guiding them. Be sensitive to each person as you pray for wisdom in leading each one who desires to be a part of a ministry. God empowers us to grow beyond what we can do by ourselves. You can help by trusting God's people to respond to the Holy Spirit in their lives.

Put your trust in the Head of the church and continue to pray for His direction. Challenge others to express their love for Christ by their service. The Lord will meet the needs for new teachers in ways you haven't yet considered. Your ministry of recruiting will be blessed and increased.

254.12   LARSON, Ellen E.
L334
         Recruiting: Help and
         hope for finding
         volunteers.

Copy 2

BETHEL SEMINARY WEST
LIBRARY
6116 Arosa Street
San Diego, CA 92115-3902

DEMCO

DO YOU FIND YOURSELF ASKING THESE QUESTIONS?

- What is recruiting?
  - What does a recruiter do?
- What does the Bible say about recruiting?
  - What kinds of people do I look for?
- How can I update my recruiting methods?
  - What new approach can I take?
- What if everyone says NO?
  - Is recruiting ever fun?

Recruiting never stops. But recruiting ideas and methods must be continually varied, creative, and fresh. This book provides many practical recruiting plans, motivation and encouragement, inspiration from Scripture, and hints to make old methods work in new ways.

Ellen E. Larson, writer, teacher, and lecturer, knows the challenging, sometimes frustrating, frequently rewarding, never-ending business of recruiting volunteers.

STANDARD PUBLISHING 18-03242

ISBN 0-7847-0232-2

90000

9 780784 702321